Long Story SHORTIES

UP TO MY LASHES IN CHILD SUPPORT

BY

DARNEATHA

Publishing Services provided by Paper Raven Books LLC
Printed in the United States of America
First Printing, 2023

Paperback ISBN 979-8-9897186-0-3
Hardback ISBN 979-8-9897186-1-0

Chapter One

"Forever I love Atlanta," they say. I say this city, or at least the people in it, can be a plague on your life if you give them enough access. If only there were a pill or a class that could properly adjust thought processes. Alas, if it did exist, I probably wouldn't be going through this shit. Steer clear, have no fear, the truth is here, 'cause that's all I will be speaking while sharing this story. We always hear about success stories from hair stylists, fashion designers, and barbers. What about an aesthetician? I don't know if it's yet to say this is a success story. I think that will be the determination of the reader's understanding about life and what success means to that individual. The goal is always success, but if it was easy, everyone would be living life in their highest preference of standard. This is a story of one's journey of turning the obstacles of life to something beautiful for life. How petty can a person be when they are triggered from changes they are watching you make? Some may think this is a story created for entertainment purposes; however, it's based on actual events.

I can start this story from before I moved out of the house I was trying to purchase for my children and me to get you caught up to current events.

I scrolled through Instagram and liked a picture on @hellobarbie's thread. "I just love how this girl is unbothered," I muttered to myself as I commented with a diamond emoji under her photo. "Let me get my ass up, get on YouTube, learn these angles, and step my game up." I grabbed my light ring out of a convenient moving box and set my phone to mirror on my television. I needed an hour of JackieAina in my life diligently. She was such a one-stop shop. As I positioned my chair in front of my mini vanity to see my television, my phone rang, and the name Ilene popped up on the screen.

I disconnected my phone from the television and answered, "Hey, Ma. How you doing?" I continued to pull out the rest of my makeup.

"Hey. I'm good. You stopping over this weekend?"

"No. I think I'm goin' stay in and learn some stuff to start increasing my content skills for social media. I want to take advantage of my time while the boys are gone. I miss them so much already."

"You not goin' out and hanging out nowhere?"

"No. I'm really goin' take my time, serious."

"You got a couple dollars I can borrow?"

"No. Why?"

"I just sent a barrel over to my husband and need to get some things done 'til my clients pick back up next week."

"You think it was a good idea for you to put your husband's needs before yours? You doing too much."

"That's my business."

"And I understand that, but you calling me makes it my business asking for my support. Am I right or wrong?"

"Girl, that school is getting to your head. I didn't have to do all that school stuff. I just got out there and built my clientele and my business."

"Look, Mama, I hate to cut you off, but I know what you did and how you did it. I was there with you through it all. Give me a chance to learn and do me in this era, please. Times have changed. I'm trying to come and add to the business you built so I gotta take it up a notch."

"If you get through it. Your patience is goin' last five minutes, Parys. It ain't fast enough for you."

"Thanks for the encouraging words. Just what I needed to hear. You know I have court with Hepatitis A and B, LaTrey's co-parents."

"Oh, I heard. We talked about that the other day."

"You amaze me how you can sit somewhere and talk about me? And with who? Let me guess. Jacqui?"

"Who else?"

"That doesn't make you feel the slightest type of weird?"

"No, it doesn't. We share a grandbaby together. That's my best friend. Regardless of what you and Jared go through, we goin' keep our relationship like it is."

"So let me just understand this. Even if they come for your daughter, you're still OK with maintaining a friendship because of LaTrey, Jared's and my child?"

"Yes."

"Did you smoke an L before calling me?"

"Little girl, don't disrespect me."

"That's the thing. I'm really not trying to, but you sitting on the other side of the fence with the opposition, what do you expect my response to be?"

"Oh, it's not that serious! You need to make amends and grow up. Take the higher road."

"You know, Mama, this is a part of me growing up, finally understanding what I don't need to be associating my time with, even if it's you for a minute 'cause you really don't understand the level of loyalty you are supposed to have in this situation."

"Get out your feelings, Parys. You goin' float me 'til Tuesday?"

"I'm not able. I have to go. You have a good day, OK? God bless you."

"Girl, you ain't thinking about God."

"Good day."

I hung up the phone and fell on my bed crying. Ilene was one person that found any window to crawl in my heart house, walk in and trip the breaker. What was so hard about my mom not understanding what I was asking her? There is nothing like the pain a child of any age feels when they lack support from their mother. I had to accept the fact my mom just showed me what team she was playing on, and it was not mine. As I cried, my heart broke to know I would not be able to have the same type of interactions as I once did with her until I was out of school. I needed to create some healthy boundaries for myself to keep my head in the game. *It's going to feel weird not coming around—that's expected—but it's weird coming around, so what am I losing?*

She needed to respect the fact that I was tired of who I saw in the mirror. I was tired of hearing my mistakes spoken about so freely, reminding me of moments I was not proud of, anytime someone felt uncomfortable when I walked into a room of people who knew anything about my past. If I went into isolation, made the necessary changes, did what was required of me to represent myself exactly as I wanted to be, what other choice would my mom have but to welcome it? It was time to walk away from everything I knew and walk toward who and what I wanted to know about myself. God would not allow me to fail.

I knew, to start and stay in that thought, it would take consistent faith and endurance to move forward and not give up or quit on myself during the process because this shit was going to be hard. I had no clue where this new journey was leading me. I just knew I wanted to be an asset to my lineage, not just exist in it.

I wiped my tears and stood from the bed self-motivated. As I re-wrapped my waist wrap, I could not help but think, *It's time to do more and say less. What is her reason?* Why did she always pick someone over me? Where did her dislike for me come from or even start? Random questions circled in my mind as I went back to watch some of JackieAina's videos on YouTube. What I couldn't do was allow that negativity to cloud my mental space while I was trying to learn how to produce better content to start posting on my socials, especially while I was in school. I needed to keep up with the girls online and offline.

I was newly enrolled in the International School of Skin and Nails, a nine-month trade program for aestheticians and nail technicians. I wanted to specialize in facials, body waxing, and lash extensions, like my mom, to work at her salon once I graduated. I liked the income I saw her make over the years, and I believed I had the ability to double and triple the income she made starting at a younger age. I thought, *If I add to anyone's salon, I'm banking on family first.*

I pondered all this as I applied primer on my cheeks and patted gently mimicking JackieAina. After finishing a light beat, I decided to get into a little fashion. They might beat me in court tomorrow, but they will not beat my outfit, Rihanna accent, and tone. I moved my phone screen to Instagram to find @ishateria. I needed a look good for court to let them know I had arrived to the occasion.

I got up to look in my closet for moving boxes I had packed the days before. I could not believe I had a court appearance so soon. The boys just left not even three weeks ago. Damn, did the co-parents fill out the application before the boys got there or what? It was the minor details my noisy ass was curious about that I know I would have never known. I just knew I needed to make a statement as I was trying on a pencil skirt that I absolutely hated with one blazer. Either it was the fact that I was bloated, or it was my emotion about the occasion making the decision. No outfit was giving me what I was looking for.

Let me find @highlowluxee for more inspiration for a look. *She is leading the girls every time I log on to her page. She is on something different and new.* "Sis winning per usual," I said to myself. "Once I get in my lane I'm going to work my ass off. There's too much I want to experience. I have to join the girls on the 'gram. I can't have the IG baddies doing it alone."

I finally decided on a look. *OK, now that I got that out of the way, let me post this face I have worked so hard on.* I looked at it again, admiring the good job I did on my blend. I went with a dark brown in my crease. My eye slant was a little higher than most and a bronzer brown to not drown my natural complexion, allowing my natural color to be my highlight.

I looked at my phone as it rang. It's CaliGurl. I quickly answered "Hey, boo."

"Hey. You got the boys this weekend?"

"No. I dropped them off to live with their dad for the next year while I finish this program and build a clientele. I want to work at my mom's salon once I'm done."

"Damn, girl. That was a lot to process. I feel like I haven't talked to you in so long. So that's where you been. Now you ain't post none of that online." She chuckled.

"No, that's my private life, that's not for the internet. Girl, yes! I didn't think I would have such a hard time processing the adjustment. It just really put me in a focused mood, you know?"

"Me and CinnamonStick were just talking about

you. I mean, we knew you weren't goin' be working at the shop with us long. I'm just glad you came through when I needed you. One of the clients came to see you. He said he tried to call you, and you didn't answer."

I laughed out loud. "I sent him straight to voice-mail. One of y'all got the money, right? 'Cause he got it. He's just so socially awkward."

Her laughter echoed my own. "Ain't they all. Girl, no, he walked out when we told him you wasn't here. We don't have natural curves like you. A man likes what he likes, you know? Sometimes they just be hella picky that way."

"Girl, I made sure I stacked everything I could before I left, and buddy that came there looking for me was the cherry on top."

"I was just about to ask you if you were coming in this weekend, but it sounds like a no."

"Yeah! I really want to get this content down for my socials."

"Now, I did see your other post. You know I'm liking whatever you drop on your socials. I'm so proud of you. You're inspiring me to find something else to do with myself. I've just been here for so long, and the money's so easy. It's just waiting on it to come in when it's slow and the time spent in this bitch."

"No, girl, I get it you don't explain nothing to me I have never judged, and I appreciate the support when

I was in the shop and online. Like, really, thank you. You a real one, sis. You know I won't be a stranger. I haven't ridden past there yet while going to the beauty supply store. You know the one I love."

She laughed. "All I can hear you saying is 'I got to get my lashes on before I start. Tell him to stay there or come back.'"

"You know my lashes are my go-to makeup. I prefer a natural face, maybe a little bronzer. If nothing else, I have to have them eyelashes on. Aww, I miss your crazy butt."

"I'm here if you need me. They calling me for a weirdo upstairs for a 30-minute session."

"Yeah! Go ahead and get that money. I'm about to get in this mirror and create some content. I just beat my face."

"OK, pretty girl, hugs and kisses. Don't be shy."

"I won't!"

It felt good to hear CaliGurl's voice. She just pushed my mood into the bad bitch zone. *I need to deliver this face. I will never judge a hustler. I love CaliGurl.* She and I had been friends for years before the lingerie shop meeting while I was dancing in Miami on weekends. Once she brought the lingerie shop, she extended the invite to help grow the reputation. I worked the evenings and weekends, when I didn't have the boys, before they left to live with their dad for this temporary stay. My doll was a blonde Amazon, standing at 5'9". She had a slim European vibe, with the longest model legs that propped up the cutest bbl, body-contoured with a long torso and 44E cup size. She blew smoke in anyone's face she was talking to without discretion, lighting a blunt as soon as she was putting one out. CaliGurl really taught me everything I needed to know to get my money, without having to fall for the sexual offers to pay me more. Working at the lingerie shop was different from working at the strip club. She knew I was a little distant and mean, and she knew I thought the clients that came to the shop were weirdos, even if they gave up the money faster.

I hated to give up the money from the shop, but I didn't think it was in my best interest to invest my time in the lingerie shop while trying to transition into my new journey. It was a commitment I made to myself and I couldn't juggle the two worlds mentally. My brain needed to soak in all the new information I was exposed to in school and my peers there. My mannerisms were completely different when I was in a hustling mood at the shop. Some of the girls there would deliberately take you off character to cut into your money kept me on guard, especially since I was highly sought after. CaliGurl didn't play about making sure I got first dibs on the new clients that came in. She pulled in her regular clients who made her at least

$10k a month, giving her the reputation of OG. It was a hustle my mom knew about from me oversharing. Once when I was tricked into thinking we were having a mother daughter bonding moment. It was only a tactic to get new information about me she couldn't wait to share with anyone who would listen.

After finally coming up with the perfect angle and taking the pictures, it was time to put a fire caption on it. I knew with court coming, the crazy ass co-parents were going to take this post personally. I loaded up three slides with a caption that read, "When you gotta make it up, but I can tell the truth." The pictures were raw—no filter, just good lighting and the perfect angles.

By the time I could commute to the court the next morning, there were forty likes on IG from the post I worked on, which wasn't too bad considering it was 7:50 in the morning. I could not believe I had to miss class to go to my court appearance. It was my first day off from school since I started almost a couple months ago, and it was the most uncomfortable feeling not being in my routine that day.

As I entered the security check in Clayton County Courthouse, the guard explained, "Keys and cell phone in one basket, please, ma'am."

The looks of the men and some women as I walked through the checkpoint to grab my keys out of the basket made it clear that I'd at least made a good choice with my look for the day. I decided on a CEO look with a Fashion Nova eggplant-colored midi dress, complimenting my size four frame with a pair of Gianvito Rossi black ribbon D'Orsay 105 pumps, my Dolce & Gabbana logo charm hoop earrings, and my girl bag to match. The heads that turned for a quick look confirmed those yoga classes were helping me with more than my mental health and stress level.

As I walked through the aisle to find a seat closer to the front of the courtroom, I heard several whispers from people who watched me, saying, "She looks like she closes cases." They did not think I was the one in court as a defendant.

The court assembled, and I looked over to my left as Jared and his wife Adrienne walked in, the sad version of the parents from the show *My Wife and Kids*. The room went blurry around Jared's 5'11" frame. He had 6'3" confidence with one bowleg. My confidence was completely out the window, even though I had resting bitch face. I didn't understand why I felt intimidation come over me when they showed up. No matter how secure I was in what I was doing, they always held my past over me triggering my fear. Their deflection game was strong, and I was so nervous that they were going to use that weak-ass tactic today in court.

I had to admit that the contrast between me now and the me that Jared knew was probably hard to handle. He'd known me all my life. We grew up together. He was watching me fight stages in life of development alone. He knew I had little to no support or encouragement; I didn't have no one to hide behind as he did. I thought his wife was slow to support his pain or whatever he hadn't healed from, but at the same time, I loved that he had someone to love him enough to share his pain and match his energy. I just wished he respected the love he received by not focusing on the love he thought he should have had with me. My case was called, snapping me out of the rabbit hole of my memories.

"Ms. Parys Germane?"

"Yes, ma'am. That's me."

"Come with me. We are going to the meditation room down the hall with the custodial parents."

"Oh yeah! The custodial parents." I stood up and followed her down a corridor.

"Ms. Germane, wait right here." She pointed to a bench outside the mediation room. "I'm going to speak with the other party first and see if they have any special requests and get their financial documentation. Then, I will present their special request to you (if any) and get your financial documentation. At the end, I will bring both parties together to determine the equitable agreement based on the information put in the calculator that determines the recommended amount. I'll present the agreement to the judge for him to sign and get you out of here back to your life in, I'm hoping, the next three to four hours." She paused and then leaned in to whisper, "You wearing that dress."

"Thank you. That could be one reason I'm in here."

I watched the mediator walk in the room while Adrienne did everything she could not to look at me before the door shut completely. I figured since I was here, I might as well take some pictures to post later. My Instagram was slowly building. I was under 2k followers with only forty-nine posts. As I propped up the phone to take a picture, I started reminiscing about how I got to court with Jared and his wife Adrienne.

When I finally realized that I needed to focus on a career I actually liked to support my children, I decided to go to skincare school to do eyebrows and lashes like my mom. It was a familiar area, thinking if I needed guidance, I wouldn't have too far to go to get it. Watching and managing my mom's salon for at least five years prior, it didn't make the decision hard to think about. I thought I could be a third-generation salon owner. My mother's mom also had a salon, but

I would be the first millionaire in the family. Not to discredit the hard work of those before me, but my hustle was relentless; it was like I had the "go get" from them both. I always wanted to be famous or publicly known for something other than shaking ass, getting into bad relationships, and fighting. I thought of it as something my family would be proud of me for having accomplished when I got it done. Every time they heard something about me in the past, it was related to some type of negative drama—I was in jail, going to jail, having man drama, selling drugs, just always into something unhinged.

The voices of their opinions and the things I knew they said about me haunted me like ghosts. On the flip side, it was motivating what my family consistently said about me. It helped me always put in a "try" to be someone they could be proud of. It seemed like I ran into roadblocks every time I came close to showing up as a positive reflection consistently. Lord only knew I was getting tired of them saying, "Girl, you have so much potential." They would hear when I broke my positive cycle. I could admit I didn't want to change for me as much as I was doing it for them, to prove them right that I did have the potential to build on. So I went and enrolled in skincare school.

The mediator poked her head out of the door and waved, breaking up my reflective moment. "Ms. Germane, I'm ready for you."

"OK." I walked past Jared and Adrienne, making sure I produced enough wind in my walk to leave my scent of Miss Dior.

"OK, Parys Germane. Do you have your proof of income?" She pulled her laptop closer with a distant demeanor.

"I do. I just started skincare school to become an aesthetician, so I'm not working."

"So what are you doing for income?"

"I am currently living off my savings from when I was an executive assistant. I do have my last two years of taxes. The letter said that was an option to have today."

"If that's what you have, sure. Are you looking for employment?" The mediator's mannerism was sketchy not as pleasant as they were before she walked in this room. I thought, *damn*. Jared and his wife were in here for twenty or thirty minutes. I couldn't imagine what piles of bullshit they dropped on my name.

"I am. I have been in this new course for seven weeks, and it's a nine-month program. I will be working at my mom's salon once the internship section starts in the course for the clock hours."

"That sounds good! Give me a minute. Do you mind staying here? I will print out the forms in my office upstairs. When I return, I will have the calculated amount and documents to go over with you and the Williamsons before I present it to the judge for signature."

"OK." She picked up her laptop, along with the documents from both myself and Jared. *I hope I'm able to work in the shop when I start interning* I thought. *My mom was really on the opposite side of the fence. It would be enough time for her to believe in the decision I made. I know now she really thinks I am doing something to pass the time in between my street hustles.*

My mother created such a very strong reputation in the city for brows and lashes, so I should have first dibs taking over the clientele. It would be a major business move for her to retire and her daughter take over. I could be her successor, retiring her from something she loved and sacrificed so much to have. I thought she would be honored to pass the torch down.

I shook my head as the mediator walked through the door with Jared and Adrienne.

"Alright, people, we should be done with this process in no time. I have father Jared Williamson and mother Parys Germane, child LaTrey Germane, age eleven. Now, with the income verification provided and given that the child is residing with the father, we are ordering the mother, Parys Germane, to pay $795 monthly."

I leaned in closer and straightened my posture. "Um, ma'am, when you looked in the system, did you see that I took Jared off child support less than sixty days ago?"

Adrienne interrupted, "What's that got to do with anything?"

I shot back, "Now is not the time. Sit this one out."

She replied, "What do you mean, 'sit this one out?' Jared is my husband."

"Happy for you, sis."

"You wish you had a sis like me. This isn't social media. This is your real life you're dealing with, not that fake one you are trying to make, stop misleading incident people."

"Excuse me, ladies. We're not here for that. And Ms. Germane, that is the number that came back from what was entered in the system."

"I can understand that. But I just started school, and they would be considered joint income. Correct?"

"You are correct. However, in this case, the Williamsons household have one income from Mrs. Williamson. Given the household expenses, the amount of the children under their care, you've been asked to pay the $795 monthly amount."

"I understand. Jared is working, though, as far as I know."

Adrienne spat back, "From what you don't know."

I asked the mediator how we would move forward with visitations, we would alternate weekends with private agreement between both parties. Walking out of the room, I was in a state of shock with questions reverberating through my mind.

I thought about my children because this was a reflective moment for me, recalling the day I enrolled in school. After I told my mom, the second thing I did was sit down with my boys and explained my entire strategy. I made sure I let them know everything so they weren't in the dark knowing it would change up the routine. I wanted them to know they were included in the process of helping me to help us. I let them know it was important for them to listen to what I was asking of my young kings. This process had to be a team effort, and from that decision of commitment to build a career. Which apparently wasn't the case if I was in court dealing with these ignorant muthafuckers, already coming at me about money.

I remember when the schedule first started for skincare school, it was so hard to balance the time out with getting the boys to school on time and making it to school myself. The boys were eleven and eight years old, an age where they could get on the bus in the morning independently. They were very well mannered and smart for their ages.

Having real time to think about the root of the co-parents' hate towards me, it wasn't just the new journey and transiting my career. It was a little bit of karma tapping my ass a little bit for moving so fast so young. *I'm too damn young to be saying, "If I would have known the things I know now," but I am saying it because I had no clue it was going to be this hard dealing with making decisions for myself with the boys so many years later.* Today showed me I was still facing consequences for having my oldest, LaTrey, with my first boyfriend, Jared, and my youngest, Kingdom, with Jared's high school adversary, Keith.

The thought of having to repeat this same deadass day for mediation with Kingdom's dad the following week just made my stomach weak. Once I obtained the documents from the mediator's assistant, I asked myself, "Why did I stop getting high again?" It was one time I needed these thoughts and this moment in the air. The drive from Clayton County to Gwinnett, where I lived, was about forty-five to fifty minutes—too much time for my mind to let this day swim in it. I wanted to stop and vent to my mom, but I was not assisting her in turning my vent into gossip. It was best to just go home and finish packing the house, removing myself from the memories of it as soon as I could.

I could not believe Jared and Keith were using the child support system to fuck with me. We had arrangements for both of them to have the boys in their care for just a year. Yes, it was an emotional decision on my part to let the boys stay with their fathers. But how could they take the circumstance and turn what could be a positive co-parenting situation into what was beginning to look like a shit show?

I mean, I was looking at these clowns as half-decent men out here in a position to hold down their children. They each got married and had more children, which was good for them. I thought it was cool that LaTrey and Kingdom were able to see that healthy, traditional family dynamic—you know, the two-parent households, home in suburban communities, with a couple cars in the driveway and dogs in the backyard.

I thought it was such a coincidence that their lifestyles were so similar, which explained why they didn't like each other in high school. These two clown manager-ass niggas had a lot in common starting with me. But why take a positive and flip it, if I wasn't a threat? Was I, and I just didn't know it? They say the devil sees your blessings before you do, but Jared and Keith weren't the devil. They were just bitter niggas still mad about a female they weren't sleeping with no more. No real power behind that to be labeled as the devil.

I loaded the pictures I took because, regardless of the day, I dressed a doll this morning. I couldn't help but wonder what Adrienne's hating ass would post, remembering her comment in the mediation room: "This ain't social media. This is your real life." I laughed, pulling out of the parking lot of the courthouse in my Acura TL. I made a mental note to keep posting fire pictures to my socials since they stayed on the front of her mind; she would not have mentioned my socials at all if they weren't. If I was a baddie, I wasn't going to stop because the shit made her uncomfortable, especially now that she made it known she watched me from the mention. I wasn't going anywhere, by any means.

How crazy is it for just wanting better for yourself, and why does it have to stir things up in people? It makes people want to cause so much tension. All this from a decision to give me a break to better myself. What do they expect a person to do? Give me the personal time to develop the version of myself I wanted to meet, enjoy her thoughts, know her interests, breathe with her in her essence of healing, joy, happiness, and self-love.

I just knew from so many years of repeating the same mistakes and cycles that I put myself in situations where I demonstrated some real uncivilized behavior with God. *I'm trying to make sure I can get down the line to the gate, so I need to have a good amount of my soul with me.* These summer seasons were not adding to the timeline. They were subtracting. I wanted to enjoy the serene side of my life as long as I was blessed with waking up that morning. I was in the beginning of an isolation period, not having anyone to really vent this shit to. *It's time to seriously detoxify all the negative damage in my soul and vent to the only person who is going to truly help me out of all my distorted way of thinking and operating, GOD.*

I have to stop caring about what others think of me and just do my thing, whatever that is, because everything I'm on now is new. I did myself a disservice for even allowing certain relationships to go as long as they did, come to think of it, starting with Jared and Keith. From what I just saw, they really didn't have any internal growth or change in all this time. They were just aging but not growing up. I mean, what were Jared and Keith thinking? They were using child support like women, emasculating themselves so badly. What were they trying to prove to their wives or even themselves?

I could honestly see where the hate was warranted. I was with them niggas in two different stages of my life, so the shit they had to say pointed to different levels of my growth as I dated both of them for about three to four years each. Jared was still in his feelings about me dating Keith, but Keith offered stability I thought I needed at the time for LaTrey. I didn't know he was Jared's adversary 'til after the fact. Jared and I were in separate high schools, so how could I? Keith was the first person to show me what a man looked like when he took care of and provided for his family. I didn't get that from Jared, even though he was an attentive dad to LaTrey and a good sexual partner. He was missing so many qualities I needed.

What was I supposed to do? Stay the same, not develop myself since I was with them? *I think not.*

As I pushed the pedal down, exceeding the speed over seventy-three, I thought about the time I wasted, and these bottom feeders had been rooting me on wanting to see me where it was comfortable for their focus. Yeah! They looked pretty good from a distance, but it's false gold. *Their childhood wounds ain't really healed.* I told myself, "Girl, stand up! We got work to do. Shit just got a little harder, but you can do anything you set your mind to! Just start trusting yourself."

Pulling up at the home I was trying to close on for the boys before the change happened, I wondered whether I should keep the crib or move forward with my emotional, spontaneous plans. There was still so much to pack. I turned the car off. My mind went to LaTrey and Kingdom because I was trying to do all this for them. I moved out here for the school district.

Their education was always important to me, and I took it seriously, trying to give them more support than I got from my parents growing up. After all, I didn't want them to resort to the other choices in life like I had to do.

Sacrificing so many of my youthful years was hard as hell, but giving away my kid or killing my creation wasn't cool to me at the time, even if I did get pregnant at fourteen. My heart just couldn't do it to my unborn child. Yeah, I was a kid having a kid. But I figured God would see me through it, so I pushed through what I signed up for.

I walked in and moved through the house, looking around at another example of me thinking I was going in the right direction with my life. I sighed and then started changing my clothes to pack up the kitchen and get ready for class the next day. Why couldn't these little boys just stick to the plan I had of starting and finishing this program without interruption?

The skincare school requirements of hours and credits that had to be met for completion were so stressful on the schedule I set up for us, but it was doable. We had a timecard we had to swipe when we arrived and when we left. We were penalized for a certain amount of tardies, which led to being released from the program and having to start over the next semester. Getting to class in the morning was very important to stay on schedule so I could graduate by a certain time. The plan consisted of getting LaTrey and Kingdom up in the morning, dressed, and ready for the bus. I had to leave twenty minutes before their bus came, so they had to wait and walk to the corner block by themselves to make the bus. By the time the bus picked the boys up, I was clocking in at school.

It was too easy to get through. *We just have to stick to the plan,* I thought as I packed one more box before taking a break to check my socials.

Chapter Two

My socials had come so far. I could remember when I finally decided to start posting on my socials. I knew a lot of people, so getting new followers wasn't hard. My phone contacts alone were over 400. Even though I didn't talk to them often, they knew who I was. I started with Facebook first to get the family involved. *They are country ghetto, but hey, that's what it was going to be. You can't pick the family you're born into. It's automatic love.*

It took some time out of fear, but shortly after I started posting on Facebook, I converted the Facebook traffic to Instagram. Instagram can be a little intimating, but if you're going to do something, give it the 100 it deserves. I was a little socialite, which helped, so every time I went outside to mingle, I asked whoever I encountered to follow me on the 'gram. My page really went up after I posted a picture of the makeup

I did on myself during my last time in Miami. I had to dance for a birthday party at one of the strip clubs. My mom's clients had a lot to say in the comments about my work being similar to hers, which planted the seed in my brain that I just might have found my hidden talent. I gained 1,000 followers and over 400 likes within three weeks, and I just kept posting from there.

After checking the stats from the pictures I took while I was at court earlier, it was time for me to retire. My brain was exhausted. Before I dozed off, I started crying, recalling an incident that happened the last month the boys were home that started the domino effect of redirection. The pain was still so fresh as it directed my memory to…

That morning, it was raining really bad, but the morning routine was still in place. I left the house a little earlier than usual, knowing traffic would be heavier. The boys had to leave and wait on the bus. Yes, it was raining and lightning, but the show must go on. We lived in a cul-de-sac, so when the bus came, the boys could run up the hill to catch it, as they did every other morning.

When I got home that afternoon, everything started off normal until I received a phone call from a social worker, calling to inform me she was en route to the house for a welfare check. My jaws dropped to the fucking floor. What the hell was going on? Now, yes, I smoked weed in the house—hell, it's my personal space—and yes, I drank alcohol socially, but a welfare check? That's pushing it.

At that time, I didn't have male company at the house when the boys were home. I learned at a younger age through trial and error that exposing my kids to my dating life wasn't always in their best interest. I had taken them through some bad experiences with my old niggas that I no longer wanted them to go through. As I matured and developed into a better mom, I didn't want them to have a lot of reflective emotional traumas, knowing I would hear about the ones they had already experienced. I knew one thing about Jared and Keith, they would help in making sure the boys knew and remembered the worst about me. There was no need for my actions to continue in helping them do that.

The caseworker arrived at the house and walked in, asking me questions about our routine and schedule. It felt so *First 48*. As I answered the questions, I thought about what could have bought this bullshit on. Like, out of all the past dysfunctional parental moments I had had, that they probably should have been called in on, what had I done that I wasn't doing then? Well, come to find out, the boys were pissed about getting on the bus that morning in the fucking rain. They went into the school having a whole meltdown as if they were abused.

Now, let me paint this picture for you as I was answering the questions and speaking to the social worker. I was making sure their food was cooked before they got off the bus and the house was cleaned. They didn't have a house chore outside of cleaning their bedroom and taking the trash out. I was taking freshly baked cookies out of the oven literally talking to the case worker. I thought, *Lady, I'm wearing my real motherhood hat with these boys, like a ghetto Clair Huxtable.*

I was just glad I didn't have time to roll that L like I wanted to. That day in particular I wanted to have the boys' food cooked and the house cleaned up before I got comfortable and started studying for my first exam. So, the lady definitely walked into a clean, well-furnished, four-bedroom house with a finished basement with a basketball goal and a fenced-in backyard.

The caseworker read from her notes, saying, "Kingdom's teacher spoke highly of you, stating that you were an active parent in the boys' education. Look, things happen, so once I verify your character from your personal references, this will be behind you. No worries. I don't see anything here that would make me think your children were in a harmful living environment at all."

I thanked her and told her I'd never put the boys in a situation that would hinder their development. She had nothing to be concerned about. As the lady was leaving, the boys were getting off the school bus. Both their eyes got as big as quarters looking at me, like I was going to knock their head off their shoulders on sight as I should have. I felt deceived to no end, as if a part of my soul left me. The case worker was like the parent police just left, I had way more rights than wrongs when it came to them. I did everything to make them happy boys. The only section missing was their extracurricular activity like basketball or football and I can blame my work or hustle schedule.

I didn't instantly attack them with the whys or the how could yous when they came in. I honestly went and smoked one to get my mind together, figuring out my approach. First I had to think about my actions. Was it a build-up from all the other times when they should have been called? What in my actions could have caused their response? I wasn't going hard enough to create the lifestyle I truly desired. What could be changed in the current schedule to add more work?

I know once I got out of skincare school, I would be making the money to get the help I need to get them to their individual activities while I worked. They just had to be patient during this school process. I was living on savings, so we had a budget to live on for a little while.

I always held myself accountable first as their parent. There was always a reason for the way a child reacted or responded to something, and I wanted to find out what it was. My love for my boys extended to the point I would take full responsibility for whatever their reasons were. Being their mom, I learned the depth of love for them where I saw no wrong in what I created. They were the perfect part of me. It was like taking ownership for their mistakes just because I wanted nothing less than the best for my children. With these thoughts, I drifted off to sleep.

With a heavy head, I woke up the next morning at 5:30 a.m., a morning routine I started when I began school, I was glad the previous day was behind me. I prayed and meditated before I introduced any other energy into my day. Four out of five days a week, I did yoga or some type of cardio to help retain the information I learned. It helped my anxiety and put my confidence on ten when I walked around during the day.

YouTube was my motivational/inspirational teacher. While I made my mushroom coffee and got dressed, I listened to those I admired, taking in the good points to apply if I needed during the day, and it encouraged me on how to show up on my socials. I was going to keep these early morning rituals going. Little did egg-in-the-face Adrienne know, I was on my journey for a better me alone with no support and all doubt in the ability to stay committed. The version of myself I held onto was becoming dead weight. She had to go. I had to keep killing the old version of myself, the one that was not for my highest good, as I told myself in the mirror that morning, "Parys, your life was supposed to be bathing in the sunlight. No more dark clouds, pretty girl," as I added a top coat of lip gloss.

Driving to school that morning, I thought about visiting my mom this weekend, but it was taking a gamble on my positive thinking streak. I was manifesting my new life. Nothing could break my focus if I was able to control my influence. I didn't want to have a bonfire in remembrance of all the shit I used to do, but when it was time to catch them up to what was going on with me in school, we would have a funeral.

Court was the following week with Keith, and she had enough gossip to conversate about from Jared's appearance yesterday. I didn't have the head space for all that. It was going to be another lonely weekend, but I was in an emotional safe space. I didn't want my situation to be the topic of gossip moments after it was shared with my mother in confidence.

I pulled up to the school so happy. This was one place I forgot about everything I was going through. It made me see the bigger picture of the opportunity in front of me, leveraging the industry coming out of school and putting my skills with my mom's. I would be a millionaire by thirty, only three and a half years shy.

Bringing in new trends that I learned from school and my classmates from other countries was going to be so bomb. Being around the multicultural students exposed me to so many different nationalities. I had a peer from India teaching me brow threading techniques and another classmate from Europe telling me about a theatrical makeup school in Ireland I could take the following summer. Clearly, this industry was bigger than the hype Atlanta was giving. Hell, if I was good enough and applied myself, I could take my family history in this industry to another level. I had my mom so heavy on the brain, I called her when I left school that day on my way home.

"Hey, Ma. How are you?"

"Hey. How are you doing? I was just thinking about you. I figured you were busy upgrading your lifestyle. Ain't that what you posted? I like the picture 'cause it was you. Funny how people forget where they came from so fast."

My mom comes straight for your neck. She ain't as bad as Blac Chyna's mom, but they would get along well. "I was just calling to check on you. You OK over there?"

"I'm good. I'm short, so can you send me the light bill money? I will float it back to you by the end of the month."

"Yeah, Ma, I can. How much is it?" I would feel guilty if I told her no again, and I had it to give.

"Oh, just $284."

"Check your Cash App." I knew she doubled the amount since she had to ask me twice.

"I heard you and Adrienne had words in court yesterday. They said you were ordered to pay almost a thousand a month. I mean, that's a little bit, and you ain't even been to Kingdom's court appearance yet. Damn, they getting you together."

"Why didn't you call and check on me? Make sure I was emotionally good? Yeah, it's higher than I expected. I had to use the salon tax returns."

"Oh! So you were making enough working the front desk with me, but you wanted to be greedy and use your body to make more at night shaking ass. What are you goin' do every month? Dance, Parys?"

"Ma, you really be on me. No, that's not my plan, sweetheart. Do we have to go here? I was in that era where, yes, I wanted more money then. If I dress a certain way, my kids gotta do the same. It's called upholding an image."

"Girl, nobody care about stuff like that."

"You right, Ma. Nobodies don't care. But OK, Ma. I love you. Let me get through this traffic. I need to focus."

"Love you too. Thank you."

"No problem."

My music reconnected through my speakers. *Damn, it's like I have to buy her love or kindness and get bad service in exchange. She's going to help keep my mind on my mistakes but never talk about what she did to contribute.* As I drove, my mind drifted to how I met Jared when my mom and his mom moved in together.

I have known Jacqui since I was eleven; she was always opinionated about me. She always dissected me. My mom and dad had already planted the seed of dysfunctional behavioral traits that I displayed from their uncultivated understanding of life for themselves. And then Jacqui watered those planted seeds from my parents, highlighting any imperfection I had. I should not have been expected to know anything in comparison to an adult about carrying myself as a woman. Instead of seeing an innocent vessel to mold into everything about themselves they always wanted to be, my youth was targeted for destruction.

They poured all their insecurities, doubts, and traumas into me, temporarily healing themselves of their damaged wounds. I was always the topic of discussion, and anything I had done recently or in my past was told to any new person I met. They wanted me to be the negative center of attention to keep what they were not doing as parents off of them. There were so many things as adults they did that was straight bullshit for women with children.

I was not one to judge because that's God's job. We all will fall short of perfection, and mistakes will be made in the learning curve of life. Now that I was closer to the age they were during my young age, I often wondered why they wouldn't have wanted me to be their protégé, equipping me with the abilities they were unable to use when carrying their visions forward positively.

Just that quick conversation with my mom had me questioning why it took so long for me to notice that my self-esteem had been under attack for a long time. The responsibility from my mom was next to none as she didn't protect me. She contributed to my ass having such a slow start to the other side of life, that life I was seeing I wanted now.

I noticed as I entered my young adult years that females my age and even younger knew more than I did in terms of building an empire for themselves so they didn't have to work as long or hard. They were more self-aware than I was in getting it done for themselves and not for people who were using them. Instead of not liking them for what they knew, I commended them for where they were and what they knew. I was glad they had positive influences and made better decisions than I did. We all couldn't be hindered from a good life.

My mom and Jacqui came off like haters toward me. They were bitter old hos we laughed at. They both needed a couch and some therapy, talking to someone to help them gain a better understanding of the shit they didn't know. But, shit, it was probably too late if they weren't willing to accept the information.

Anyway, thinking about what my mom said, yes, the co-parents were getting me together. It was a nice amount I was paying for LaTrey, and I hadn't got to Kingdom's case yet. Maybe it would be in my financial best interest to take my ass to the lingerie shop this weekend, lock myself in there for the weekend with my study material with me, and work. I could create some cute, educational beauty content surrounding what I learned in school this week. I asked Siri to call CaliGurl.

She answered in her normal greeting, "Parys, France," with a German accent being silly.

"What's up, baby! I'm locking in for the weekend. I need room to work." I used our code for "send some of the other girls home so I can get most of the clientele coming in."

"Say less. You OK?"

"Girl, yes and no. Jared got me on child support."

"You got to be shitting me! What in the fuck is he on?"

"Right?! He's on something, ain't he? It's like $800, and I have court with Keith next week. I want to put a little more up, you know?"

"Girl, yes! They are absolutely disgusting for doing you like that. But you know I got you. I got your guy's number, and I will let him know you are coming in to work to make it easy for you. I will make room so don't worry. You coming from Friday to Sunday or Monday?"

"Sunday night, so I can be ready for school Monday."

"I need a facial, and I got two others that need a facial too, so bring a kit and charge them $150 each."

"That's my doll, bet. And you know you can tip me for your facial or, better yet, dinner."

"Yeah, baby, you need to run it up this weekend—no

sleep. The boy's dad is trying the shit out of you, and you trying to move your mind differently, you know? On something positive, that's crazy! I hate to see it! Let's get you in and out of here."

"You always read my mind."

"I know what type of time you on Parys. I'm here to see you win. Some of us ain't built to be in the life forever, and you one of them."

"Thank you, per usual. Let me get my mind ready, and I will see you soon."

Before CaliGurl hung up, I heard her scream, "Parys coming to work this weekend! Order the bottles. Skittles, I need you to take off."

When I got home, I worked on packing the house and started brainstorming my content ideas to create for the weekend. I decided to create skincare routines, waxing techniques, and brow/lash application videos with whatever trending sounds were circulating this week.

As I went into the weekend, I couldn't help thinking about what my mom said about my post. It wasn't just Adrienne in her feelings about my captions. It was my family too. My page gave me the image of a developing beauty technician and aspiring influencer, the glow-up was throwing them off. They knew the Internet could literally change my life overnight.

As I worked on the content for the weekend, I knew

I had to go hard on my videos. I always had in mind it only took the right person to see my work or the potential of what could be. I was posting to build my own clientele whether I worked in my mom's salon or not. I kept my head down, working on everything I planned for myself, and by the time I looked up, it was the following week and the morning of court with Keith.

I woke up that morning praying heavier than any other morning. The day felt strange for some reason. A lot of that, I can't deny, was due to knowing Keith was more dramatic than Jared, and he would put on a show if he was ever called to the stage. I thought, *Let's go with a Fashion Nova pantsuit, white, with a nude bodysuit I ordered from @hellobarbie's site with my nude So Kate Christian Louboutins.* My gold LV hoop earrings paired with the LV wristlet scent of the day would be my YSL Libre. If I had to endure the foolishness today with Herpes Simplex Virus 1 and 2 and miss another day of school, why not look and smell amazing?

I had to travel to Fulton County today, which was where Keith lived and where he filed his application for child support. The Fulton County Court system had a known reputation for being ghetto. It was nicknamed "the revolving door"—you came in and right back out for any charge. People had been known to sign their own bond for even shooting someone. The system was so overpopulated and the cases were so backed up, they really didn't have the capacity to hold anyone or handle any new cases.

When I stepped in the courtroom, the first two I saw were Keith and his wife Justine. I moved my eyes to the row directly in front of them and caught a glimpse of a familiar body frame. It was Jared. I could have fainted—at least my spirit did—but I had to save face even if I was screaming inside. I know Jared wasn't there for moral support. What kind of reality show scene was I seeing here?

I found a seat and got comfortable, but my mind was in shambles as I recalled the last incident after the caseworker came over for the kids and the fight that happened later that night. I heard the boys in the other room arguing. It was nothing too unusual so I didn't get involved. I yelled from the other room, "OK, calm the fuck down and get it together, guys." They quieted down a little.

Then, fifteen minutes later, I heard a full-out brawl, and LaTrey yelled, "I hate you! I wish you were dead."

I immediately ran out of the room to see what happened. They both had their own rooms, but they were in LaTrey's room. I walked in, screaming, "What is goin' on? What's the problem?" They were arguing over a game, and I thought, *You wish he was dead over a game?* I didn't play with throwing negative words toward one another. Those words were like cussing. I taught them that words were powerful, and direct negative words were NEVER used around them or toward them from me.

I didn't know what or where this level of anger came from because, at this point, LaTrey was in tears, yelling, "I hate it here! I want to go stay with my dad!"

Those words emptied a clip in my chest! I couldn't believe what he said. I grabbed his slender body with no thought and slammed him. We went behind his bed as I continued to punch him, hitting him in his chest and wherever else my punches landed for at least three minutes. I stopped in tears, upset at myself for coming out of my character, not keeping my shit together with my kid. LaTrey was my first love, my reason for being.

I pulled back tears, coming back to the present moment.

"Parys Germane?" The court mediator was at my side.

"Yes?"

"Can you come with me to the mediator section?"

"Sure, I can." I stood up to follow her out of the courtroom.

As I walked by the other people in the various rows,

I heard, "Damn, she fine. I would have done what needed to be done."

The mediator continued as if she didn't hear the bystander. "Parys, if you can sit here 'til I speak with Mr. and Mrs. Coleman, then…"

"Excuse me, yes, I am aware of the process today. I'm taking time away from class today, and I would like to move this day along to get back to my routine. Thank you kindly."

"Oh, OK, no problem. I will be right back with you and will do my best to get the document before the judge to sign."

I didn't see Keith or his wife, assuming they were already in the room. When I looked over to my left, there Jared stood, staring out the window. When I looked at him, all I saw was a walking flesh wound, just a bitter-ass man, lost in his emotions. I was never a hater. I firmly believed in moving in the direction that's right for you, but do yourself some fucking justice. Don't drag your past with you.

Jared never took time to find out who he was for Jared, and I got it. I know what he had to work with being there. He lived with his mom, basically unemployed, until he was twenty-one, when so many of his peers had surpassed him. When he ran into Adrienne, he saw that girl as a come-up, so he played on her insecurity to get what he wanted out of the relationship:

stability, comfort, and love. He had to play his cards and use every play he could, even if it was his little baddie baby momma that he wasn't completely over. Adrienne's background was a lot different than Jared's or mine.

I could validate that while our moms were on their bullshit, Jared and I were together, nurturing each other to cope through it. I couldn't believe this nigga would take time out of his day to be here for Keith when I once saw him trying to fight the man in our driveway. He loved me to the point of hatred, befriending a former enemy who also once loved me—it all seemed dysfunctional and psychotic. *What does this case have to do with Jared?* This was confirmation to me of what I had always known. Jared kept the grudge and resentment toward me that actually worsened after I had Kingdom. Anything negative Jared could say about me around LaTrey, he would, so he needed to build all the evidence he could as a fucked up mother.

"Parys Germane, I'm ready for you."

"OK. Thank you."

As I walked by, I heard Keith's wife, Justine, whisper, "She's goin' be working for us."

"What did you just say?" I stopped in my tracks and locked eyes with her.

"I'm not repeating myself, and I'm not Catrina. I'm not scared of you."

Laughing, I replied, "Oh, he sold you on my old reputation too, I see."

I flipped my bob as I continued to walk in the room on the mediator's encouragement. Once she closed the door, she immediately said, "Look, I don't know what you did to this couple, but clearly, this is past the child support for Kingdom Coleman. I had to redirect the conversation numerous times to my position as a mediator for the Department of Child Support in Fulton County, not a counselor or a therapist."

As I listened, it was obvious that Keith came in that room spitting fire about me. Poor lady, it was clear she was stressed. "Ma'am, I know the type of hostile energy that just came at you. And on his behalf, I apologize. You just want to do your job. I know. I'm not going to waste your time. Here you go." I handed her my information, along with the order from Clayton, hoping it would be considered.

"Thank you," she said as she started entering the information into her computer with urgency. Still typing, she added, "They are trying to speak to the judge about strict visitation and stated you had a situation at your home where a caseworker came out to take Kingdom."

"Excuse me?"

"Mr. Coleman stated Kingdom had to come live

with him 'cause you were providing an unfit living environment."

My mind froze, and I couldn't process her words. I was literally watching damage being inflicted on my reputation and possibly documented in the court system. I could not believe what I was witnessing. All I could do was go through the process and focus on my goals and avoid unnecessary distractions. The best way to beat that foolish behavior was to ignore it. The first time I responded and showed them attention, they would have control, and I wasn't going to give it to them.

The mediator prompted, "Give me a second. I'll be right back."

"Yes, sure. Take your time," I managed to mumble. I needed time to reflect on what the mediator just said. I needed to make sure my head was in the game.

As soon as she closed the door, I leaned back and grabbed my LV wristlet off the table for my lip gloss. I turned my camera on from my phone to make sure I lined my Bratz Doll puckers perfectly as my mind went back to that night with the boys 'cause, apparently, I was still suffering today from the repercussions of jumping on LaTrey. After it happened, I called Jared to share what his son said. I wanted to see how he felt about it. I tried to hold back my tears so he could understand what I was saying. He answered on the first ring.

I blurted, "I just jumped on LaTrey about his attitude toward Kingdom over a game, and he said he wanted to come live with you."

"I mean, if he wants to, that's cool." Now, take into consideration this was happening fifteen days or so before the school year was ending.

"OK. The school year ends in about fifteen days. Are you OK to start summer and take him for a year?"

Now, this man owed me child support and wasn't paying consistently. The weekend visits were once a month, if at all. The visits would all depend on whether he and his wife wanted to emotionally extend themselves to deal with Jared's "past mistake" (LaTrey was once referenced as).

The questions he answered with ease were more to taunt me than to really support his son. Whatever his reasons, I planned to take him up on every word he said without question, holding him accountable, making him stand firm. This was the first time I had ever called Jared about LaTrey with a behavior issue.

Jared continued, "It's time for LaTrey to spend more time with me. He's getting older. It'll give you the time you need to better yourself like you want. We'll work out the details as we go along, but, yeah, it's a go. No problem."

"OK. I'll talk to you later. Thanks."

Hell, since Jared was taking LaTrey, I wanted to see if Keith would take Kingdom. I thought if both boys were gone, I would have free time to work my ass off. In all fairness, they were eleven and eight years old. I gave Jared and Keith years to establish their life to their satisfaction without any interruption. Maybe it was time for them to return the favor, so I called Keith.

While I dialed the number, Kingdom approached me. "I don't want to stay with my dad. I'm good where I'm at."

"Oh, no, it's only fair. It will only be for a year. Let's just see what your dad says." I was much calmer when Keith finally answered the phone. "Jared is getting LaTrey for a year, and I need you to do the same. He is giving me a chance to get completely on my feet without interruption. You know I just started skincare school. I have a lot of work to do." I knew Keith was not going to let Jared out-man him in any area, especially when it came to me. The rivalry had been that way since high school.

"Yeah, I mean, I got a lot goin' on here. We just found out we're pregnant again. But, I mean, if you are in that type of need, yeah, I guess so. When is this supposed to start?"

"At the end of the school year and for the following

year. I want to work out the same visitation schedule I have with Jared so I can have the boys at the same time."

"Yeah, that shouldn't be a problem. I guess we can talk about that then, but call me back later. I'm at work."

"OK."

As I set the phone down, Jared's home number flashed across the screen. All I could think was he was changing his mind, so I didn't answer. It rang again two minutes later. I answered reluctantly.

Instead of Jared's deep voice, I heard the whine of his wife. "Why are you doing this to me?" she cried in my ear.

"Excuse me?"

"Jared just told me that you asked him to take LaTrey for the next year, without asking me. You disrespected me by asking him and not both of us."

This was the first time I had spoken to her in over a year. The last time was at LaTrey's birthday skating party, where she made a point to be as antisocial as possible, eventually starting an argument with Jared, accusing him of looking at me periodically while I brought out the cake. They left early because she decided to cause a scene and Jared cussed her out. She'd just had their daughter, so I blamed her behavior on the hormones.

"Were you home when I called the first time?"

"Yes."

"So why didn't he extend the conversation to you so you were involved?"

"Your call was intended to disrespect me."

"I understand how you feel because it is a big decision, but that is your life partner. I wish he would have included you in the first call so you could have had a say in the decision. But it's already been made. Where is Jared?"

"He just left."

"Oh, OK. So you having this conversation without him about him having a conversation without you?"

At that point, I was done talking to her. I was going to let this bitch vent and get back to my thoughts 'cause I was over it. She took in my response without a rebuttal and just cried. I stayed on the phone and supported her. My female intuition just knew all those years of presenting the "perfect world" was coming to an end for her, so she was upset.

For many years, Jared didn't acknowledge LaTrey's existence. They really wanted to create the "black excellence" couple life and image. I thought it was revolting for Jared not to acknowledge his son, especially because, for all those years, he talked about men not wanting to date me for having two children by two different men. At least I stood in my truth!

Adrienne cried for at least three to four more

minutes. Eventually, she said, "I'm not helping you raise your child. What do I look like?"

"You may not want to help me raise my child, but you will help your husband raise our child whether you want to or not."

"You are so jealous of the life I have!" she yelled.

"I prefer something a little better." The feeling of guilt finally dissipated that I fucked Jared once when she was pregnant with their son before they married. "Look, girl, settle your affairs with your husband, or, better yet, y'all call me back together. You're mad he said he wanted to help me get life how I want it."

"Wait, what did he say?"

"Girl, bye." I hung up.

The memory of that conversation floated away as the door opened, and the mediator returned.

"I'm sorry that took so long. I haven't gotten used to the new construction. Our department is on the other side of the building. " The Colemans followed her into the room.

I replied, "No problem."

"So I have father Keith Coleman and mother Parys Germane for child Kingdom Coleman, age eight. I really love that name."

Keith and I simultaneously thanked her.

"I have the child residing with the father in a one-income household. Ms. Germane, I did add your other support case, but, to be honest, it didn't make a difference. I have you at $639."

Justine piped up, "Why so low?"

"Why you asking?" I glared in her direction.

"That's my wife. She can. And why is her payment to me lower than her other baby daddy? Can you run the numbers again, please?"

"Nig—I mean, boy, no."

"I got her other baby daddy here with me to vouch for anything you need to ask."

"That's the reason for him being here? Oh, OK."

"Mr. Coleman, there is no need for me to talk to anyone who is not the guardian in this case pertaining to Kingdom Coleman. Thank you. I will not be recalculating the number. It is generated from whatever is put in the system."

"Then, I need to speak to the judge about this. My son—"

"—our son," I corrected.

"I'm glad it's only one."

"That was my decision 'cause we almost had—"

Justine interrupted again, "You done had so many abortions. It wouldn't have made it."

"That man is gaslighting you, young one. He knows what this womb can do."

"Um, Ms. Germane and Mr. Coleman? Can you remain focused, please?"

Keith started fidgeting. "I need to speak to your supervisor."

The mediator replied, "Mr. Coleman, one moment," as she stood from her seat, opened the door, and gestured for the officer to enter the room. He closed the door behind him. "Mr. Coleman, this is not an appearance where you can speak to a supervisor or the judge. This is an appearance to enforce a child support order. The only one in this room who will be available to speak to the judge is me, and that's indirectly to get the order signed. Is that understood?"

"Yeah, I guess."

I sat back, enjoying the checkmate move.

"We are done here. You can wait in the courtroom or the hall for your copies," the mediator concluded as she picked up her papers and computer to leave the room.

The officer waited until we all exited before he left. I stepped into the hall because waiting in the courtroom would give me anxiety and the urge to stop on the block and pick up seven grams of a loud pack.

Walking out of the courtroom to wait, there were Mad, Madder, and Maddest standing in a circle, venting, looking like unwanted puppies. I was so unbothered, focusing on the fact that I had just accumulated over $1300 a month in child support. I had to keep my mind together seriously. I was glad I worked at the lingerie shop this weekend so I was up a little more.

I just wanted to quit completely, not even use the lingerie shop as a backup option if my savings got too low. I had to focus on building a good clientele with my aesthetician services and pour all my energy there. Mixing the two worlds wasn't an option for me anymore.

Not wanting to waste the look of the day, it was time to take some pictures for social media. I was definitely going to pour gasoline on the fire by taking pictures right where I stood, whether they saw or not. It wouldn't change how they felt about me anyway, so what did it matter?

I propped my phone up and then noticed a message alert from a salon owner near my school. I immediately opened it:

Hello, I'm Rachel, I own a salon not too far from the school you are at. I hope you are having a good day. I was very impressed with the content you posted this past weekend. I started following you a while back, closely watching you for a month. I would like to invite you to an opportunity to rent out a room available in my salon. I have walk-in clients available for you to service as I am now going into sixty days of being fully booked. I think the walk-ins would help you build your clientele base. I

*know how difficult that can be. When you have a moment,
I would like for you to call me to schedule an interview
day and time. Hope to talk to you later!*

I remembered seeing the salon on the corner of the
intersection by the Whole Foods I often visited during
my lunch break.

I typed a response, "Good day. Thank you for considering me for the opportunity. I am in class now.
Once I get home, I will give you some days and times
for when I am available to come in for the interview."

Somebody recognized my work. The feeling was
unexplainable. All those second-guessing thoughts I
had about myself in the lingerie shop that weekend
were so self-sabotaging. I thought I looked weird being
alone, not posing at any Live functions. I simply posted
positive quotes, random fly pictures of various outfits,
and beauty content.

But my likes were lit from the four beauty videos I
created at the shop. Notifications from the likes were
still pouring in, so why was I so surprised? Riding the
confidence boost from Rachel, I posed for more pics
in the courthouse.

"Stop fronting. You a camouflaging-ass rat. You
ain't influencing nobody." Justine sneered at me.

"You a fan? I'm not signing autographs today.

Matter of fact, would you like to come take this picture for me?"

"Bitch, you trying it."

Little did she know, I was trying it. She was calling my stupid, and I was about to answer, knowing I could sign my own bond. But then I thought, *Parys, no*. I did not want Keith's ego to swell thinking we were fighting over him. She would have been, but I sure wasn't.

"Girl, ain't no way you should be thinking you popping. Both your baby daddies put you on child support. They hate you, and your kids hate you too."

I set the timer to capture another pose. Flash. In my peripheral vision, I saw Keith and Jared laughing, dapping each other, as Justine turned toward the bathroom. After one more picture, I grabbed my phone and started heading after her. I was curious if she was as tough one-on-one as she was in front of her husband.

Before I could reach the bathroom door, the mediator stepped in my path. "Ms. Germane, here are your copies. I wish you the best."

"Yes, thank you." I shook the lady's hand, trying to catch Justine before she exited the bathroom. I was cool until she mentioned my kids. I needed her a little uncomfortable, but everything happened for a reason. Who knew what would have happened?

I walked toward the elevators, walking as if I was

having a Savage x Fenty runway moment, whispering to Jared and Keith as I passed.

"Y'all be blessed."

Chapter Three

When that elevator closed, my head started to hurt so bad. It was as if I ran into a wall. I was over dealing with Jared and Keith at that point. The way I was watching them used the system to trap me was annoying as fuck. I started negatively dwelling in my feelings about LaTrey saying he hated where he was and how he wanted to stay with his dad.

Justine's words felt like confirmation. I had to resist the temptation to get depressed about them as the feelings started brewing. Justine's comment shook my tree a little. I couldn't lie; I loved my boys. These innocent children had no clue they were being manipulated. It was sad as hell to know their fathers had started taking advantage of their immature minds. They were too inexperienced in life to know that the pain, disappointment, and revenge that their dad had toward me was being passed down to them.

Jared and Keith demonstrated the mentality of, "I hate her. My child will too." Jared's presence at court today brought to mind one word: unhinged. He could get his flowers in terms of the time he spent raising LaTrey. What he was unable to do financially, he made up for domestically. Jared potty trained LaTrey. I didn't. I worked and made the money providing child care, clothes, and food for our son, and, yes, I was gone many hours after school hustling 'cause one of us had to do it. So, it's fair to say LaTrey had a good bond and relationship with his dad, as I thought every boy needed. LaTrey looked up to his dad. I just really noticed when Jared moved on from his feelings toward me, he expected his son to do the same.

In my attempt to keep the co-parenting arrangement peaceful, I didn't call out every incident confirming what I saw or felt. This extreme dramatic-ass moment today made me regret not calling the bullshit out on sight every time, but, damn, didn't that deplete energy from the bigger situations I needed to address? The wellbeing of our child was my focus.

I stood on the court steps for a minute to collect myself. Jared planted so many seeds in making his kid hate being home with his mom, all because it wasn't his home with his dad. Jared pulled that narcissist shit toward LaTrey, showing he didn't like him if he showed any happiness with me.

It was apparent the day of the incident because, for the first time, I saw Jared in LaTrey. I saw that hurt little boy Jared once was toward his mom when we were growing up. What I witnessed that day was not the heart of my son that I knew. It was the influence of an individual from my past who didn't care to see me grow away from him. Even if he was a married man with other children! It was like watching the devil's spirit use my son's flesh, and that thought alone froze me where I stood, stuck in silence on those court steps.

How could a person be so heartless toward their own child, wanting them not to love the womb from which they were born because of their personal feelings? Was picking a side that serious?

And Keith was an open-and-shut case. He was mad at me for a different reason. I left that relationship due to his verbal and physical abuse. He assumed his gifts made up for his behavior. By the time that drama was added to my life, I was twenty-one with two children. I wanted more for myself at that time. *I now understand why people either stay the same or move to a different city because changing in the same city with the people you were raised alongside is hard to do peacefully.*

I finally moved my feet and walked to my car. A fire lit inside of me. I was on child support for both the boys, paying three times what they were paying me when they were on child support. They only had the boys a couple of months. It was time to work a little harder on myself and develop a solid plan for turning this around. Otherwise, this situation was going to drive me crazy. Thinking about the positive side, Jared and Keith gave me the time to become consistently stable in a career I enjoyed. I had that. Now, I had to do something with it.

It was time for me to take myself down the path of enlightenment, not just for myself but for my boys. I wanted my children to see that the world was theirs to create whatever they wished. They just had to want it badly enough, know that they deserved it, and apply the pressure. God would give them every clue of the direction to take. They just had to make sure they didn't fall for the distractions or listen to the noise around them. I wanted to show them how to quiet their mind, take control, and keep control, but I had to be that example for myself first. It was time for me to speak up for myself more and show up as the person I was fighting to become all the time, not only when it was convenient. I knew my purpose was bigger. The situation and people in my life were very determined to make sure I didn't advance for some reason.

I needed to start standing on some necks, making people uncomfortable, exposing the contributions that influenced some of the bad choices I made so we all could be involved in their gossip. I was tired of them just pointing the finger at me when, so many times, it was we.

I was no longer saving the feelings of anyone blatantly showing me they gave two shits and one fuck about how I felt. I was matching energy! It was time to rack up these successes so they could talk about them just as loud as they did my failures.

As I pressed the gas pedal, I turned on Marvin Sapp's "The Best In Me." I sang along with the song. *I am better than the rumors. I am better than my mistakes. I am better than the unfortunate events I experienced. I am better than what I have been called. I can learn more. I can be disciplined. I can forgive myself and forgive others, I can be understanding and honest with myself. I hold myself accountable without judgment. I am all that God says I am, and I can do all that God says I can do. I will fall short, but I will pick myself back up and keep moving as long as I have air in my lungs. Every day, I give myself the same chance to try again, just as God did. I have thankfully reached the point of wanting a change for myself, recognizing that I needed it.*

Pulling up to my house, I decided to have a mini-photoshoot moment. I wanted more pictures on my pages. First, I would load the ones from today with a warning shot caption now that it was confirmed, for a fact, muthafuckers stayed watching my pages.

I created a lash beauty video with slides transitioning

to the final looks. I showed one side, which was almond-shaped, and the other, deer-shaped, and explained which options complemented different looks. The lighting was perfect, the way I explained the difference was relatable, and the visuals were chef's kiss. I crafted the caption, "See, the power of the mind is not a joke," as a throwback spin-off quote from the song "Both" by Gucci Mane featuring Drake.

I spent about a solid two hours from start to finish. Not even five minutes after I posted the video, my notifications went crazy. I waited until I finished packaging boxes, took a bath, and climbed into bed before I checked on the response. I checked the comments and the stats. I expected the typical 200 likes on my Instagram and a little over 100 likes on Facebook. Boy, was I in for a surprise!

My post had over 5,000 views, over 800 likes on Instagram, and well over 200 comments. I jumped up and down in my bed. Somebody would have thought I was four years old. I was stoked! People messaged me with questions about when I was getting out of school, if I was already in a salon, if I was working with my mom, and if I could work out of my house. Some even asked if they could book with the school and request me.

Then, I opened Facebook as the band played while the *Titanic* began to sink… Why would someone be messy enough to share Adrienne's post? Of course, it had to be someone in her circle entertained with the gossip they heard about me. It was just too childish. I didn't read the details, knowing they would make me mad, but the message read along the lines of how her husband's baby mother motivated her to be a better mom for his children. She was glad God blessed him with the opportunity to have more children so he could experience a good partner and mother to his children, blah, blah, blah. It also included information about the social worker's visit to my home. I had to wonder how she heard the details of *that*. Then, I thought, *Jacqui,* as I scanned through the post, shaking my head.

My mom and family seeing my work added more drama. Anger quickly turned to sadness. Not one of them liked my post, and they made up 30 percent of my followers. I wasn't upset—just disappointed. It would have meant the world to me to see them chime in with the strangers. They knew more of my history and were watching my efforts to better myself firsthand. What was the harm in pressing a fucking button on an app? Was it that painful to see their family doing good?

Clocking into school the next morning, I had to keep it a stack. My family not supporting me still weighed on my mind, while the views doubled overnight. I knew I had to start posting more. I had fewer than 130 posts between both pages, and I hadn't even started building on TikTok or YouTube.

Usually, I wasn't into posting everything I did. I always thought attention was a hell of a drug. I wanted to post with a purpose. I wanted meaningful attention. The beauty videos gained the greatest attention, so I had to build more content from there. The increased views boiled my creative juices. Every move I made from then on was an opportunity to create content. I titled this next chapter of my journey, "Shit on 'em," as I focused on the vision of a successful future.

It was time to showcase my capabilities without a thought or concern of who was uncomfortable. I remember one of the comments from a follower on my Instagram wondering whether they could request me at school for services. I asked my instructor that morning if clients could request me once I reached the hands-on part of the curriculum. That was five weeks away. After receiving approval, I posted a status of when I would be accepting clients during my school hours. The likes flooded in as my alarm went off to remind me to call Rachel to schedule the interview.

I scheduled the interview for my lunch hour two

weeks before I could start servicing clients at school, which would give me enough time to settle in the new place. I couldn't help but think about the boys. They would be starting school around that time. Thank God I dropped the boys off with an extra-large box from U-Haul filled with new clothes, shoes, their favorite toys, etc.

My mind drifted back to the day they left. Jared and Keith met me at my mom's salon that day. She was a block over from Martin Luther King Jr.'s house, directly across from the natatorium. My mom turned the property into a work/live space. She worked out of the main sector of the house and leased the attachment to a hairstylist and masseuse. The location was a neutral spot to kill two birds with one stone.

Well, Jared pulled up first, of course, with his family in their suburban truck, just one of their many cars. Adrienne's jaws dropped when she saw the box coming out of the back seat of my car. I asked Jared to help get it out.

"When will we hear from you?"

"I'll be in touch in a couple days to get a schedule together. I plan to downsize and move to the north side."

"That's about an hour from us."

"Yeah."

This level of communication from me was nothing I

got from him. They never gave me that much respect as a co-parent. I noticed as I talked, Jared's body language indicated he knew I was on some real grownup shit. I set the tone for this co-parent interaction during this process, hoping the nigga would take notes so when LaTrey came back home, he would step his game up. I wanted him to see I was not the enemy.

Adrienne honked the horn for him to wrap up the conversation, yelling out the window from the driver seat, "Don't forget. We got to be there at three."

Jared's facial expression said otherwise. She was just saying that to get him to hurry up. She didn't want him looking in my face too much longer. He always had a look in his eyes when he saw me, like he still loved me and hated it.

Keith was a different story on the exchange. He pulled up alone in one of his Cadillacs, playing his music loud, like we were still in high school. Gold teeth and a polo outfit gave him the Carlton look from the *Fresh Prince of Bel-Air* but from the south side of Atlanta. I could only think to myself, *Out of 8 billion baby daddies on the planet, this is what I once did.*

"What up, shawty? We got to talk about how much you goin' give me every month."

"Excuse me?" The audacity of this simple leprechaun when he had not been off child support for a warm thirty days at that time was already asking me this bullshit. "Damn, you quick, ain't you, player? Pipe that down. We goin' figure it out." I had a flashback to Keith Sr. making this same play on Keith's mom when he got child support from her. Yuck!

"Yeah, 'cause, shawty, you know my expenses goin' up helping you."

Apparently, he saw my child support for Kingdom as extra income to his household, and he was thinking about additional income for this whole process.

"I'll call you in a couple days to talk. I gotta go."

The reflection of that day made my heart so heavy. I just wanted to work, right the wrong turn I took in my life by letting my boys go to their dads, and silence these feelings and thoughts in my mind.

For the following two weeks, I posted beauty content from school, moved into my new place, and created motivation/inspirational videos. Looking from the outside in, I looked like I was busy and focused. I started studying different lash techniques and brow styles. I bought a mannequin head and practiced in the evening for hours. I lived off what I saved from the lingerie shop and felt uncomfortable even thinking of going back in their hustle. I wanted money from this industry even more than I saw my mom make at the height of her focus, producing over $100,000 a year. I kept my head down with the task in front of me, and by the time I looked up, it was the day of the interview with Rachel.

I wanted a light makeup beat face to narrow Rachel's focus to my knowledge and negotiation skills. I was very confident in my gift of gab; I was naturally a people person in business. When I got to the interview, I was impressed with the spa's visual aesthetic. The location was at the forefront of a small plaza by a busy intersection with the most amazing amount of sunlight. The bright light shining through the window from the street brought so much attention to the contemporary aesthetic décor of the salon, immediately calming your anxiety within seconds of exposure.

Rachel, at least fifteen years my senior, wore a tightly fitted scrub set with a glam beat face. She resembled Janet Jackson to me, wearing the cutest jeweled studded Crocs. I could clearly tell she was into her personal image, which was different from how my mom was as a salon owner. When my mom worked, she didn't care about how she looked. I remembered her wearing the same jean overall set like a uniform for at least three to four days a week during her first couple years in business. Looking back, now I can laugh because that shit was so savage.

Rachel welcomed me warmly. "Your Instagram gives you no justice. You are really pretty. Those ain't just good angles or filters, I see. You are actually prettier in person."

I didn't know if she complimented me or if she came for me, but I wasn't focused. At least my picture game was on point.

"What are you bringing to the table?" she asked.

"A social media presence, 'cause you don't have one." I had a little room to pop my shit with the success in consistency from posting my content. My accounts had grown over 15 percent, even though I was still trying to figure out TikTok's algorithm.

"Arch Me clientele are above social media for growth."

"If that's what you trained your mind to believe, I'm here for it. But this industry is too trendy for you not to make sure you stay tapped in, tuned in, and turned on."

"I like the way you think, rookie." Rachel offered me a 60/40 commission split, which I knew was a slap in my face. I was still responsible for 50 percent of my supplies. I negotiated a 65/35 commission. Once I got involved, I would become a complete asset and add growth to her existing business. I offered youth and new beauty. The industry always welcomed a fresh face or look, and I was confident I was going to bring it.

I wanted to learn from Rachel too. She had the experience I needed, and I had knowledge of the new trends to add to her business. It was a cute collaboration if you ask me. Rachel was completely in love with my spunk and was ready to move forward with me the following month. I asked her for a contract in writing, including a ninety-day revision, knowing I wanted to eventually pay booth rent to get her out of my pockets.

Walking out of the meeting on my way back to school, I envisioned myself as a future leader in the industry. The energy of Rachel's salon was upscale with diversity in her clientele. She played spa music, offered refreshments, wore a uniform, and did not take cash. Once I left the interview, I posted a status. And what did it do? Go up! I let everyone know I would keep them posted on my start date and when they could schedule appointments once I got settled. After the interview and the post, I began to see a different outlook about what I was doing. It was the first time I felt the feeling of accomplishment from what I was doing on my own. I was proud of myself.

After school, I was sitting in traffic when I received an unexpected call from a lady I worked with, dropping off pounds to belles of weed periodically, some years ago through my mother's salon. She was a Jamaican named Jamaica, of all things, and she had long dreads that she always kept in a rolled crown covered with a luxury branded scarf like Burberry or Chanel—always a dope look.

I answered the call, "What's good, goddess?"

"Shit, come through."

"Yeah, I'm en route. Let me get through this traffic."

When she called, I knew what it was about. Even though I wanted to remain focused on strengthening my craft and educating myself in the beauty industry, I knew I could work with her once a week and have enough to last me a month as long as I budgeted. I was trying to change, but I was not going to leave this type of money on the table.

I met her at her house on the east side of Atlanta. I hadn't seen her in a while. I forgot how sick her body was as she walked to the door, so sensual. Despite her being 5'0", her presence gave her proportions more like 5'8" 32-24-42.

"Hey, sexy lady," I greeted her with a hug. "It's so good to see you."

"You're too beautiful. Come in. Have a seat. You know I don't do small talk. I got some moves I need you to make. How far are you willing to drive, and what's your schedule for school?"

"I will drive where the money is. I go to school

from eight to one, and I start working at a salon in a couple weeks. I'm thinking the hours there will be from two to seven."

"Oh, yeah! I just saw that on Instagram. I love you on socials—super cute. Congrats! My friend said she been to that salon before. It was by her job. I mean it wasn't your momma's work, but she was cool, though. She complained how long the wait was since she only takes walk-ins on certain days."

It felt good to see I was being watched and noticed, and the salon had a reputation of being busy. It definitely kissed my spirit when Jamaica said it.

I replied, "Schedule me for the night or evening drives. The boys are with their dads, so I'm up and outside whenever."

"Your car good? The service up?" Before I could even respond, she passed me a wad of bills, what looked like $1,000. "Make sure you got everything you need. Within a couple days, you should be hearing from me."

I kept my face blank as I looked directly in her eyes. We exchanged seriousness and focus, but between me and you, I was screaming inside. I left and figured I'd take myself to dinner afterward, flexing my band on the Instagram and Facebook Story. I reflected on this good day as I ate dinner.

My socials were attracting people who wanted to help me, as well as ones who didn't like the changes I was applying to my life. I had to start being mindful of which side of the spectrum I would give attention to, the positive or the negative. I admitted to myself I was so focused on the negative shit and the reactions, I was missing the positive moments, like the two from today alone. I missed my boys, and I knew that time was coming to call and arrange to get them soon. I could not process they'd been away for the past three months, but I couldn't selflessly admit that the self-discovery road I was on was nice.

I definitely wanted to do more soul-searching to learn who I really was and what I was capable of. It was the first time in my adult life I didn't have kids. It was just me. There was no one to consider, check on, feed, dress, etc. I was doing well with the adjustment, thankfully keeping my mind on my craft, school, social media trends, mediating, working out, and praying. Yeah! I was doing it, but I still had a ways to go.

I had to accept it was also my healing time. People don't understand it is hard to simply erase the voices you've heard for so many years. Sometimes, my mind replayed the most painful remarks as a routine from not hearing them in a certain amount of time. It's like getting yourself unstuck from pessimistic glue. The most common mental replay was, "Don't forget where you came from." The memories resonated too deep. Hell, how could I? It was just the fact of me not wanting to go back where I came from, but as they say, *If the devil can't keep you distracted, he will keep you busy.*

Damn, I was having a slow moment because it took too long to figure that out. I was slow like a lotus flower blooming out of muddy water. Did my mind have to be quiet for me to hear that? Hearing it earlier in my life, I might have paused a lot of things I welcomed in my space, even if it meant cutting off family ties.

Over the next few weeks, I kept my head down and my routine going. On the day I started working at Arch Me with Rachel. Thoughts rambled in my mind as usual. I felt healed enough to at least start making friends at school. I was cool with my classmates but kept my distance. I didn't grow up having a lot of friends.

Being pregnant at fourteen and having a baby at fifteen, life directed my attention away from being too social. I was put out of high school and transferred to an all-pregnancy school, which was a psychological mind fuck, if you asked me. I was in a relationship with Keith by seventeen in our own house living as a family with LaTrey, who became my best friend for many years after Jared. I knew a lot of females but never had the time to make lasting friendships. When I did observe female friendships, all I saw was a lot of gossip and betrayal. I only had time to focus on the wellbeing of my children and myself.

The only other example was my mom and Jacqui, and that wasn't motivating. I never saw anything positive from their dynamic. I moved through skincare school knowing everyone's name but not knowing them personally. When they extended themselves too much in my space, I always felt uncomfortable. It really wasn't from anything they did but more so me not wanting to be open and expose my flaws or imperfections.

As my socials continued to grow, so did my popularity. The clients from Instagram booked me at the school. This change was both good and bad. I looked busy, but all that moving around wasn't making money, only tips. Still, I was building my clientele. I set a goal to establish a reputation before I graduated from school so I could take that clientele with me. I was on track to say the least.

I posted about the clients I provided services for while in school, keeping the interest up while gaining new followers, which looked inviting and welcoming. The only elements missing from my social media image were friends within my same industry. I looked around the courtyard at my classmates, wondering, "Can I trust these strangers? Let me push myself out of this comfort zone and get a little more friendly."

I first thought about who would fit the vibe. I couldn't lie. I needed to be honest with myself and point out the fact I had trust issues and barriers to overcome, but I was going to try. I talked with a gay guy named Prai more than anyone else. Prai was a dark chocolate, slim-built, and well-polished guy who always seemed to be looking in a handheld mirror when in conversation, as if he was practicing his angles when talking to people. Seriously, the boy had the face of Raul Paul and the old Michael Jackson from the *Off The Wall* album.

Prai had a girlfriend he met in school named Foreign, who reminded me of a light-skinned TikToker, Aliyah'sInterlude, that alternative black girl look. She had a vibe like the girls on the show *Euphoria*, even in her choice of clothing. We all spent the last four—almost five—months going through the course together. So I decided to start this friendship journey with the little familiarity I had with them.

Mingling with other aesthetician friends in my industry would show me being sociable, adding a different perspective to this public image I built for society's standards. They were on social media a little, from what I saw after doing my homework to make sure I made the right decision in new friendships. I wanted to surround myself with positive people and vibes. I needed some iron-sharpening-iron energy, and plus, this was social media, where your chosen friends could make or break you. My followers were growing, and I wasn't going to damage it. I had the opportunity to build a new life from the ground up, and I wanted to do it right.

After lunch that day, I walked over and started small talk with Prai and Foreign. We discussed a test we'd taken earlier, and we all experienced the same feelings of nervousness and anxiety about the results.

I asked, "Y'all want to get tacos and a drink after class today? We could end the semester on a celebratory note, with the test we passed."

They issued an easy collective, "Why not?" and we agreed to meet at the Mexican restaurant in the plaza by the salon. Yes, I planned to go to the salon the first day after drinking with classmates. I couldn't lie; excitement filled me thinking about the money I would make between trafficking and working at the salon, in addition to passing into the next semester of the course.

We began loading up congratulation shots to our Instagram Stories and Facebook posts. What I liked about all of our platforms was we all had makeup and aesthetic posts. Prai presented himself as the correctional skincare guru. He liked chemical peels, facial products, dermaplaning, etc. Foreign was a makeup artist posting amazing makeup transitions. She had the most followers out of all of us. She freelanced with MAC for two years. Foreign was already taking clients from home, and she even had a booking link in her bio. That's when you could really start making more money. I shared with them that it was my first day at Rachel's, and they made a final call for a round of shots as a celebration.

Foreign said, "I think I remember seeing that on one of your posts. She's been there for a minute, like five years now. I know a couple people go to her and have been for years. She has a long-ass wait time, though."

All I could think about was that wait list was about to be in my pocket. Ms. Pac-Man was coming through, period! We wrapped up a two-hour lunch, agreeing to link up again soon, maybe for a concert or a happy hour after the chemistry semester, which none of us were ready for. I freshened up in the bathroom before heading to Rachel's. I wanted to at least brush my teeth and freshen my makeup to make sure I didn't look oily and/or tipsy on the first day.

I walked into the salon, and Rachel's phone rang. I saw her in the back with a client, and she yelled, "Get that! Answer it with the salon's full name, please."

Is this a test? I answered it after the second ring. "Thank you for calling ARCH ME, Parys speaking. How can I help you?"

"Yes, I have an emergency event to attend. I wanted to know if you have any availability in the next hour for a brow wax and full set of lashes."

"One moment. Let me place you on a brief hold to check on that for you."

Rachel peeked her head out from the back room. "You sound good on the phone. How are you doing today? I didn't think you were going to make it in. Weren't you just at that Mexican spot?"

"Let's focus on the lady I got on the phone. Are you able to take her in the next hour?"

Rachel gave me a look, like "OK, she on business," not able to say what she wanted to with a client at her station. "See if she is willing to see you and book her. Those calls come in all the time. I always have to turn them away."

"OK." I walked back to the phone. "I am not able to get you in with Rachel, but I can get you in with another tech."

"Oh, no. Is she good?"

"Rachel wouldn't have them in here if they didn't complement the vibes. Girl, you goin' be OK. Come on in."

The woman on the phone laughed. "You cool. What's your name?"

"My name is Parys, and I will be here waiting for you. You need 6:00 or 6:30 p.m.?"

Chapter Four

Once I got off the phone, I had at least forty-five minutes to set up my room and prepare for my first client. I went Live on Instagram as quickly as possible. My long-ass nails went click, click, click on the glass. "Help me set up 4 my 1$t client." I knew my views would boost from the title alone. After I set the countdown, I started unloading my car and checked my phone every time I came back into the salon.

During the second round, viewers jumped up to 205, and by the third and last round, I was up to 510. In the course of four minutes, it quickly grew over 2,000. The car was close to the entrance of the salon, and I was moving fast. I looked at all the comments to know how to begin the conversation while I unpacked.

Comments said: "You ain't got your room ready yet," "Where the pics on the wall?" and "It's goin' look so boring for your first client."

I responded, "Oh, I ain't got time to hang up the pictures. That's for another day. There are clients in the building. That would be real unprofessional to start banging on the wall in a serene atmosphere." The hearts immediately started going up on the screen.

Another comment read, "Girl, you doing good."

I continued to move around and explained to the viewers, "The schedule between Rachel and I only allowed me to come in one day for a couple hours, so I did my deep cleaning, burned my sage, and set my intentions. And thank you, boo. We gotta start somewhere, right? While I was in here setting intentions, I took videos and shit so when I got to the red dot boutique (Target), I got everything I needed for the décor, you know?"

More hearts floated on the screen. I ranted a little bit more before signing off Live. It was slowing me down, going back and forth to read the comments. Because I decided to invite several different opinions into my life during this journey on Beyoncé's Internet, it might be in the best interest of my mental health to always be ready and stay on top of how I moved and what I shared pertaining to my business. I wanted to stay professional and current, if I wanted to be a trendsetter.

I knew I had to find a product to sell to help me generate more revenue, and there, I started thinking about investments I could make with my money from the streets as I brainstormed, before I got shook, thinking to myself, "Girl, this ain't school. This is your first real client."

While I walked from the trash to the front of the salon, Rachel came out, explaining how to check out a service ticket in the system in the most confusing way. I listened, but I wasn't, thinking, *When I finish this client, I'm going to have to ask because she is putting too much on me while I'm thinking about this history I'm making for myself.* She probably didn't realize she lowkey blew my buzz with the "Answer the phone" move. Knowing Rachel had a phone in her room, she was trying it. I wanted something out of this opportunity that was more important to me than any bullshit she could ever throw, so I kept it cute.

When the client arrived, she had nervous-ass energy, so I knew I had to make her comfortable. Her nervousness wasn't about to wake mine up. We had to get through this process.

I asked, "Would you like a bottle of water? Do you have to use the restroom before we start? I'm going to have you for at least one hour."

"Nah, I'm good, and if you have me out of here in an hour, I got you on a hefty tip."

I first had her sit in the chair, and I took the stool behind her. I gave her the mirror. "Tell me what you want to see. What don't you like? What do you like?" I wanted her to feel comfortable expressing her preferences and critiquing herself. It was my job to enhance my clients' beauty, creating a look to make them feel more confident in their skin.

I definitely took everything she said into consideration, but now as a creator, she gave me the image of what she wanted to see, as far as the shape of her brows to how she wanted her lashes. I, of course, added my two cents to the ninety-eight she gave, and that pushed her to the 100. Once I was done, I gave her the mirror again. She was so in love!

"Can I get you on IG?"

She enthusiastically responded, "Girl, yes, brows and eyes only." I took a picture, no filter, and uploaded it, and it immediately blew up with likes and comments on both platforms!

I loaded Boomerangs to my Stories during the process, building up for the post. Strategy succeeded! Even if they didn't support me, I still wanted the family to see the work I produced.

I left for the night, only able to service one more client, still with multiple slides to add for my "first day out" post. Once I wrapped up, it wasn't even two hours before my phone rang from Jamaica asking me if I had to work at the salon that coming Saturday morning. She wanted me to leave in the morning for a day trip.

I told her of course because I was only working weekdays at the salon for the first month. I was definitely in on the day trip. I redirected my route to fill my car with gas before heading home, counting the $5,000 in my mind before the day even came. My routine for the remainder of the week stayed the same, and I produced eighteen new posts of clients I serviced within the first week working. Before I knew it, Saturday was here.

I woke up, prepped the car, and uploaded all the movements on my Instagram Story without the gritty details with a lit-ass song. I made it safely to the address, made the drop, and heaven blessed me on returning back home. Back in the city by 5 p.m. that evening, I stopped at the store to get more things for the new content ideas I thought of while driving.

I posted to my socials about "how you never know the life you can have 'til you experience the life you lost," thinking about the boys. If they were home, I would be taking them somewhere nice or buying them something they really didn't need but made both of us happy. You know I did a little dance with the stacks from the drive, saying "Don't play with me, bitch. We getting money. Where y'all at?" on my Instagram Story to feed my ego and shake the sadness growing in me from missing the boys.

Well, in came that black cloud. It wasn't even the

Tuesday of the following week, and it was like Adrienne had time to let her anger procreate from little mad to big mad because the direct messages started that morning at 6:15 a.m.

She wrote, "Can you call me this afternoon 'cause your son need things."

Now, when I needed shit, I couldn't call these muthafuckas for nothing. They were on their own wave, like I was supposed to be right now, but this bitch knew how much I loved my boys. She knew I would respond.

I texted Jared with the screenshot, asking, "What's the tea? What LaTrey need?" I got no response. I waited until after class that day before I sent another text and still got no response. I told myself if I left work without a call or text response, I would just try to call this nigga because at this point, it was just a bother.

Adrienne could really pick someone else because they picked LaTrey up with a box of shit he needed. I knew they weren't out of food because her thick ass was not missing any meals. She was on demon time from lurking on my page being nosy. Let a doll build. I would not leave my kids out of nothing I had going on. I was doing this for them.

I waited until my shift was over when I called Jared back. That was my last time trying to call. Jared saw me on his line. No need for a text. We're adults. I was responsive and reaching back out. Who would have known that this social media thing was really going to get on people's nerves this bad?

Well, I wasn't stopping. I was cool and collected in my feelings. When the table was turned, I didn't have views to watch from a social media perspective. I personally watched them grow and was happy for them. Long story short, I was glad that even if it was after me and with another female, Jared and Keith were some decent guys representing family life with somebody's daughter.

I carried on with my evening after that third and final attempt when I received a call from Keith. Now, this clown wasn't sugarcoating none of his feelings.

I answered my phone. "Yep?"

"You on your socials showing out, I see. What you got for Kingdom? You glowing up, leaving your kids behind, like a bum-ass bitch. What you on, fam?"

"Bro, what in the fuck are you talking about? Does Kingdom need anything? Don't call my cellular device with this bullshit. As a matter of fact, where he at?"

"In the other room."

"Put him on the phone. Let me check on him real quick."

"I called you. I need to make this real easy for you to understand. You've been on child support two months. I only got one month so far. Jared said—"

"Have Kingdom call me when he needs something. Get the fuck off my line."

After I hung up, I looked in my Gucci bag for my blunts. I got a sample from Jamaica for moments just like this. I needed one in the air. I had a feeling this was just an introduction to new bullshit because of my posts. After I scheduled my content for the next couple of days, I remembered why smoking was probably not the best idea with these emotional ups and downs 'cause my thoughts became too deep.

I moved every year or two all my life, literally never having the same address for more than two conservative years. I wanted stability. I commended what Jared and Keith did in their lives for their kids. I wanted the same. I started to cry, thinking about the shit Keith called me on and how I knew he wanted my energy with the drama. What I wasn't going to do was put my energy into nothing that wasn't aligned with the goals I set. Jared, Keith, and their wives were knocking on my stubborn door, and I was going to let them in.

Was their depth of hatred for my personal development and growth so intimidating that they watched and studied me to see what area in my life was the weakest to target in their plot for my demise? What about me sharing my personal happiness triggered them to come against me that didn't trigger them with someone else online doing the same? Or was it the fact that they had access to me through my children? Was I oversharing my happiness and pride in myself, completely forgetting and/or disregarding pain that others might be still experiencing?

When people witnessed or shared time with you in a dark moment of your life, sometimes it was difficult for them to see you healed. I got that. But why should I be concerned, focused, or fearful? I was doing the internal work. I acknowledged things about myself that I didn't like and started changing them to better represent the woman I was becoming. Why was I not able to share that for the world to see without feeling like I betrayed my past? Why keep my heart in discomfort and my growth and belief limited to their standard and not my own?

I fell asleep that night mentally exhausted, making up my mind to ignore them. If my kids weren't calling, asking for what they wanted, it was a Do Not Disturb for Jared and Keith.

I worked and remained in my routine for the next month after that night. It was hard, though, because I was only able to speak to the boys once out of the eight times I called. There were always excuses—they were busy, playing outside, eating, cleaning up.

Adrienne even told me one time, "LaTrey on punishment. Jared said he couldn't talk on the phone."

"Excuse me?"

"Look, I don't want to get into y'all's business. Can you call back once Jared gets home?"

I felt like her attitude toward me stemmed from my social media. It couldn't have been from anything else. During the lost time, I made two more Macon trips, I posted about three to five new clients every day from the salon, I was getting more recognition from school, and I even started shopping a little more. I loaded up pictures and reels with me at Lenox buying the boys clothes or things for their new room, posting how I couldn't wait until they saw their gifts with at least four to five bags in hand every time. I know the big Louie bag sparked a fire under someone's jealous pot, but that was not a concern I needed to bother myself with. I worked for the things I was getting in my life, not even really sleeping to get it. New clients continued to message me, wanting to know where I was located and how to book as I directed them to the salon.

I even started getting male fans, asking if I was dating anyone. One in particular was an Internet comedian I followed named Direct. I threw some comments on his posts, and he reciprocated. We exchanged hearts, just some light social media flirting. But I went no further. I was in my routine, and it was working for me. I didn't want to mess anything up.

After I left the salon one evening, I received a notification from IG. A quick glance revealed that it was a brand. I wanted to wait until I got home to open it, taking my time to read the whole message. I walked into my apartment, counted my tips from the salon, read a chapter from my aesthetic homework in preparation for a test, drew a bath, and created some content. When I climbed into bed, I saw that a lash company wanted to work with me on a paid collaboration! I was so excited, I started jumping on the bed and screaming, "Let's go to work!" I didn't have anyone to share the moment with, but that didn't lessen my enthusiasm. I decided to share it with my growing online community.

I was talking to the almost 2,000 viewers for about an hour, answering questions while drinking a glass of wine and smoking. I received congrats, hearts, and even a direct message from Direct that I ignored. In my feelings, on the third glass of wine, I started crying, thanking God for opening doors for me, and keeping my head leveled during this process of growth. This quickly spiraled into an entire praise break.

"God, thank you for listening to my heart and being the governor over my prayers. Thank you for trusting me with this new assignment, continuing to guide me and protect me from harm seen and unseen, opening doors that no man can close, and allowing me to go through this path, keeping my feet moving forward, not backwards. Thank you in advance for the blessings you are giving me that I haven't seen. I trust your word over my life 'cause your word will never return void."

I was starting to see the life I would have had, were it not for having the boys so young. I felt restored. I felt the emotion and finally understood after all these years what my grandmother meant when she said, "If you don't give that baby away, you goin' stop your life."

I can't lie. Regret came over me, not regret toward the boys but regret over the choices I made and not being able to make better decisions under the circumstances as a kid. Yes, I had no control over my living arrangements, but I had control over the choices I made in those living arrangements.

I wanted to call my mom so bad, but I didn't because I suspected she was at the bottom of her feelings from what I'd been showing online. So my focus went to the terms the lash company wanted as I was ready to sign the agreement. They wanted two reels and two posts on my page for ninety days and one Story a week for thirty days. Yes, it was a lot of work, but I picked up $3,500 and a major brand on my building résumé. I knew this brand also opened the opportunity to become visible to other brand collaborations in the future. It was a done deal.

Talking to Prai and Foreign the next day, I was a conversation piece. They spoke about how refreshing it was to see that side of me, especially when I was in tears.

Prai asked, "You didn't feel uncomfortable?"

"No. That was how I felt in that moment. I'm learning to love the things I once hated about myself. I'm a beautiful soul, even with all the flaws. I want to share myself more. That alone would make people want to come get services. No shade."

Foreign added, "Girl, deadass. My eyes got watery. That was good shit. Your words were organic, and you showed so much transparency. Stay focused, sis." Her words validated me. She continued, "Sometimes, I have the same thoughts. I just keep them to myself."

"Thank you, boo, but I need some help from both of you."

"Yes, sis, what you need?"

Prai looked in his handheld mirror. "As long as it doesn't involve my coin, we are good."

"I want to find two models. Prai, I need you to do their facials. And Foreign, I need you to do their makeup so I can concentrate on brows and lashes for the brand. I want to hire a photographer to do a three-hour photoshoot and get the ninety days of content I need to produce."

I planned to pay everyone for their services and time.

Prai and Foreign replied at the same time, "Bitch, yes! Let's go!"

I posted a "get ready for collaboration" post, tagging

Prai's and Foreign's pages. Then, I put out an ad looking for models and photographers. Once I left school, I stopped by Whole Foods and picked up a salad on the way to the salon. I was in a good habitual consciousness of what went into my body. The yoga and the diet had the waist snatched, which offered such a confidence boost.

When I arrived at the salon, I set my bag in my room, only to hear the door open again. I turned around to see Adrienne walking in on Facebook Live, apparently having a conversation with her viewers. Behind her was another lady I didn't recognize. She was dressed professionally, so I assumed they weren't going to fight or attack me.

Still, I wasn't sure. Rachel looked over at me, completely startled. My jaw hit the fucking floor. I approached them to prevent them from bringing their drama any farther into the salon.

"Bitch, what is this? Why are you at my job?" I said in a low, direct voice.

Before I could utter another word, the lady behind Adrienne asked, "Are you Parys Germane?"

"Girl, yeah. You know who I am. What's up?"

"I'm serving you a civil suit for child support."

"A civil suit? I'm already on child support. How bored are you?"

Adrienne threw in, "Oh, yeah, throw that on your Live feed!"

Rachel rushed them both out the door. "OK, you all have to leave. This is a business, and I have clients in the back." She then turned to me in disbelief. "Parys, what you got goin' on?"

I stood in complete silence, confused and embarrassed. "Rachel, I apologize. I have no idea. I'm as confused as you are."

"Honey, wash this day. You have to get this sorted out. After I close up, I will call you on my way home."

"I have seven clients scheduled."

"Reschedule them for your next available day before you leave." She closed the door to return to her client.

I was relieved that she didn't mention firing me. I rescheduled all but two of my seven appointments, as they didn't answer the phone. I left them each a detailed message that I would be unavailable. When I finally got in the car, I cried in embarrassment.

I was in a rage at how they caught me off guard at the salon. I wanted Adrienne's head off her shoulders for coming to my job with that bullshit. The fucking audacity! There was no way this monkey-brain-ass ho was not going to feel heat on sight when I saw her. The maturity was out the door for me. I didn't give a shit about how I was going to look after this square up. I needed that smoke.

My IG rang. It was Direct. What perfect timing.

"What's good, little momma? How you doing?"

I wiped tears away, getting my face together for the perfect angle and lighting, "I'm good. Just dealing with some unexpected bullshit leaving work."

"OK. You good? Look, I'm not goin' hold you long. I'm outside linking with my bro about doing a skit. I'll drop the addie. Pull up on me. I'm tired of chasing you. I'm ready." He wasted no time to shoot his shot and didn't allow me a chance to decline.

"Boy, you ain't been chasing nobody," I said with a flirtatious laugh. "You know what? Go ahead and drop the addie. You can get some time. This may be the distraction I need tonight."

"Bet, where are you coming from? So I know how long I got to finish. You need my undivided."

"North side by Perimeter."

"Oh, OK. Don't be no more than thirty. What's your Cash App? Stop at the liquor store for us. What do you drink?"

"Mostly champagne or tequila."

"Most definitely on rich bitch shit. I got you. Come on."

I sent him my Cash App information while on the phone, and he transferred $150 with a message "hurry up" before he disconnected. I wanted to call Jared's ass on the way, but before I could dial, Keith called. I looked at the screen like it was possessed.

I answered, "What?"

"Oh, you already know my paperwork is coming next."

"Nigga, you whack as fuck. I need to spend time with my son this weekend. As a matter of fact, where's Kingdom?"

"He's right here. Before I put him on the phone, know that paperwork should be coming to your momma's house since I haven't got the new address for you. You online doing the most, abandoning your kids, thinking you glowing up while your kids are suffering and watching."

I burst out laughing. "Keith, you sound delusional. Send him to me this weekend. I've been calling. You been avoiding. Knock it the fuck off."

Kingdom's voice came to me then. "Hey, Ma. You moved already?"

"Yes, love. How are you doing? Look, I need you to stay on your dad's ass this week so you can get to me this weekend. I'm goin' work on LaTrey too so we can hang out."

"OK. Love you." I heard Keith ask Kingdom to hand over the phone while he was still talking.

"Look, I'm outside in public," I explained as I

approached the liquor store. "I'm gonna be at my momma's house Friday at 6:30 to wait on him."

"Yeah, that's cool."

I hung up as I opened the door and I had to call my momma.

"Ma, why did Adrienne come to my job today with a civil suit for child support court?"

"Oh, she really went through with it."

I stopped in my tracks and turned back toward my car. "You knew this shit was about to happen, and you didn't tell me?" My chest constricted in excruciating pain.

"You knew enemies were coming for you, after all the blessings you've been showing."

I just listened, but I didn't want to hear anything positive she used to gaslight me.

She was covering her tracks for her next question. "Are you able to float me a couple dollars for the shop's phone bill 'til next week? I just covered the rent."

"How much you need?"

"$185."

"OK. I just Cash App-ed you. Let me move around real quick. I'm about to have people in front of me. I can't talk like I need to."

"Thank you, darling. I love you. Be safe."

"Always. Love you too."

I couldn't let her dig that hole an inch deeper. I

blazed up the L I rolled once I got in the car on my way to Direct. I rejected one of his video calls and responded with a message instead. I really had to mentally collect my shit before I saw him.

The ride on the other side of I-285 helped me release a little tension as my mind floated into thoughts about why they would make this process more difficult for me than it had to be. Jared and Keith had taken on a competitive spirit with me. I didn't have the same energy toward them when they made necessary moves and decisions to set themselves up where they were in life. Were they worried that I would supersede their accomplishments in my time alone?

This was an opportunity to put myself in a good position for my boys. I was lowkey trying to match the wave they were on, so I wasn't looking like the falloff parent. I felt like I could be a better me for the kids. They deserve to see that from both parents.

And I ain't got the energy to address my mom at this moment. All of that was a lot to digest at once, but the ride helped me deescalate my anger from earlier. It simply fueled my motivation, and I thought, *Go harder*.

Chapter Five

When I pulled up to the address Direct sent, there were a lot of people on the street. I called him to let him know I arrived. He walked out, actually not as cute as his IG pics, but that was cool. The Palm Angels track pants with a clean white polo shirt with his Yeezy Boost 350 pulled him together enough to still call him fine as he walked toward my car. I wasn't at my typical ten that day either. Given the day I had, I went from a ten to a fucking eight. I pulled up wearing a white Dundas yoga onesie with a pair of white Air Max 97 sneakers and some lightly tinted Gucci glasses because my eyes were puffy as fuck from crying and my lashes were sticking together.

"Hey, little momma. What took you so long? I been finished. I thought you ran off with the little Cash App. I was thinking, damn, I have more than that to give."

I giggled, knowing that as a comedian, he wanted

to start with something funny. "Boy, no. You know how traffic is. Plus, you sent me on an errand. "

"Never that, love, my bad. And you right. I could've had someone else do that for us. It's my first time over here. I wasn't pulling money out and doing the most. This is the West End (an urban hood in Atlanta). You know it be the ones right by you lurking. You never know who watching."

"Facts."

Direct got in my car and said, "Turn back around and go that way. Now that I finally get to be around you, I ain't sharing no time with nobody else. Let's park and talk, have a little late dinner, and you can drop me off at my high rise."

"Well, don't you have it all planned out, cutie."

We parked, rolled a couple blunts, popped the bottle, and had a decent "get to know one another" conversation. He took my mind off all the drama I experienced that day and all the shit I knew was coming. When I first started talking to Direct, I noticed he asked me questions in sequence. It was like he had so much curiosity built up in his mind that any opportunity to ask me questions, they came out of his mouth like a torrent. My first thoughts were that he was trying to figure out how to play with my mind, learning every detail so he could know how to line me up in his category of women. I thought, *Mr. Sir,*

I'm going to tell you what I want you to know until I can trust you. Hell, I have too many dark secrets that can be used against me. I wanted to make sure while I was potentially coming out of this break into dating someone that I made better decisions than the ones from my past.

I watched him for a while, at least the last year, periodically. I saw him collaborate with other women for skits but never anything personal like couple pictures, date nights, or vacations. It made me a little curious as to what his type was, but honestly, he was silly. The nigga made me laugh when I needed it, keeping me company plenty of days and lonely nights with his posts.

Don't get me wrong. The 6'2" in height, 220 simple build, with neck and arm sleeves was sexy on that Godiva dark chocolate skin. He was givin' every bit of bad boy with a sense of humor. I could have done away with his dreads, though. They were really not to my personal liking, but hey, that's what he liked. His fashion sense kept my attention, though—metropolitan chic, or it was just "the Capricorn" aura about him. He was always in the latest and most current drip, which was not a surprise. He had over 800,000 followers on IG and 1.3 million on TikTok, so he had to keep it on at all times. There were too many eyes on him.

I turned to Direct, passing him the L. "Let me ask

you a question. And you have to answer it without too much thought or ask me a question as a response."

"What's up, loveface?" he said, slightly smiling with a head tilt. He tapped the ashes off with his finger.

"Why do you ask me so many questions at one time? Like before I can answer the first one, you on the third or fourth question."

Direct laughed out loud. "Aw, Parys, that's too easy! I thought you were about to ask me for my health portal login information for my clean bill." We both chuckled. "'Cause I was just about to say I ain't got one. You goin' have to trust me, and I ain't got what you ain't got." We both laughed harder.

"You are too funny. And we goin' table that for another time. But seriously, Direct, why you do that? Is it just with me, or you just like that?"

"No, Parys, it's just with you! You kind of like a mystery to me, after watching you for so long online, trying to get to know you from what you post. You hard to read. I really still don't know enough." He paused to stare at me deeper with his brown eyes. "You guarded like a mofo, doll, like whatever you've been through in the past ain't getting back in. I mean, it's cool with me. At least I know you ain't Internet buss it open ready." He inhaled from pulling on the L. "But I told myself, once I got in to where you trust me, I for sure was goin' ask what I needed to, so I have to figure it out 'til you trust me and just freely talk to me. I want you to trust me with whatever that brain of yours is thinking about." He grabbed me by the back of the head to pull me forward to place a kiss on my forehead.

"Awwww, Direct, that lie sounded so sweet. Where you pull that from?" We both laughed.

"Girl, you silly, deadass. You in a safe space 'cause I don't want you to go nowhere. You wasn't easy to get to, and I don't see it being easy to lock your ass down either. And I'm cool with that 'cause Daddy got plenty for you." He passed the L back to me. "I just got a funny feeling your love is goin' feel different, like real love that I won't be able to replace, 'cause you really don't care who I am or what I will become from a social standpoint. Feel me? You are not into my status quo."

"You right. I don't care about that. Just put me first. Don't let no one change your mind from the personal experience you have with me, turning you against me or doubting me for nothing. I want my next man to stand up for me in front of anyone, let them know we are rocking, and protect my name at all cost, you know?"

"Nah, Parys, I can feel that! I got us—no embarrassing moments. That ain't even hard, at least not for me." The champagne was putting thoughts in my mind during the conversation. I heard Keith's words in my head. It was annoying, but in reality, those doubters were going to have to get accustomed to the glow-up because I was just getting started. My new successes motivated me to want more, as they were supposed to. I wasn't slowing or stopping myself because it made them uncomfortable. What kind of self-sabotaging shit would that be?

My personal issues weighed down so heavy, it blew my appetite during dinner, so I took my pho bowl to go. And it didn't help I responded to a text from Jared. He asked me if I wanted him to drop LaTrey off at my mom's when I picked up Kingdom. How in the fuck did he know I was going to be at my momma's house to get Kingdom? They had to have been talking to one another. Of course, I remembered Keith said earlier, "You know my paperwork coming next."

As I drove Direct home, he talked. All the while I wondered whether he had a car or not as we pulled up to his high rise.

"Get out and give me a hug, lil' momma."

"OK." I walked around to the front of the car, and he held his phone. Holding it over the both of us, we both smiled.

"What's good, y'all? This is the new me. I'm claiming, so my guys, if you're shooting shots, you can stop 'cause I just won the game."

We both laughed. I looked at his views. There were over 15,000 in a matter of two or three minutes.

I blushed and clouded my mind with thoughts of, "Where is his car at?" He talked his shit on IG Live, which I'd seen before, but the fact that I was included this time was cute.

"To my sneaky little links, don't call me 'til I call you. I ain't fucked yet, but I know she got that stay down."

The hearts and laughing emojis flashed across the screen. I don't know if it was the attention on me, but I knew that when we linked up the next time, I wanted to look my absolute best.

I rode home in a glow as my notifications on IG kept dinging as a result of his Live and Stories. He locked it in with the quick picture posted on his page, with the caption, "If she don't think I'm goin' make her mine, she slow." So cute!

I missed a call from Rachel, but she called after 10 p.m. I was on personal time. I planned to call her in the morning on the way to class, and I took my exhausted ass to sleep!

I woke up a bit earlier than usual the next morning. I needed to clean up the apartment, burn my incense, read my Bible, do my yoga/meditate, and set my intentions for that day. When I walked out the door, there was no telling what type of music I would be dancing to. I wanted to be spiritually protected and mentally prepared.

I called Rachel on my way to class.

"Girl, you know my salon was all over that girl's page and lowkey went viral."

"No way!" I went to Adrienne's page to see how much damage was done. I knew Rachel was not big on social media. She was one of those "out the mud" businesses. Much like my mom, she built 80 percent of her clientele from word-of-mouth business and showing up every day. Adrienne's video had over 400 views.

"One of my clients sent it to me, asking me who I had up in here with the ghetto drama. That's not the image or reputation I have established for my salon, honey."

"I understand, and on behalf of myself and Adrienne, I apologize for my personal situations even making it to the salon. I was completely taken by surprise."

"Oh, it was obvious from the look on your face."

"I deadass didn't or wouldn't have ever thought anything like that would come north of Atlanta. Not that bullshit can't happen anywhere, but you know what I'm saying. She wanted a show, apparently. I didn't even know it was posted on Facebook. That's even crazier." I couldn't wait to get to class to do a little more investigating. The square-body bitch didn't have IG, so I didn't have to look on too many platforms.

"Do you expect this to be a frequent thing?"

"I hope not."

"Me either. If it happens again, I'm going to have to let you go. It's just beneath the quality of clients I service and the brand I have built."

"I understand and respect what you are saying. You are not supposed to handle it in any other way." I pulled into the school's parking lot.

"OK. I scheduled you five additional clients for the evening. Since I'm leaving early, I need you to lock up this evening."

"Well, damn, OK. No problem." I was wondering whether she looked at my books.

"I really like you working here with me. I think you are going to be amazing, girl. Handle your business and leave that drama to them low-vibrational people. You're better than that."

"Thank you, sis. I needed to hear that. I got you."

My conversation with Rachel forced my mind to think the hours I spent in school could be put toward working and building my clientele. I wanted more exposure at the salon. That little move Adrienne pulled was definitely a tactic to fuck my image up and what I had going on building my profession. While she was trying to prove something about my image, I had to fight to prove it wrong by producing more of my best work every time. I didn't give a damn about what anyone thought or had to say about anything from my past. The old me was dead. I was relentlessly showing the new me, and they were seeing it firsthand.

In class, I worked on model selections and negotiated the rate for the photographer. The shoot was the Sunday of the coming weekend. I didn't want too much time to pass by. I was excited that the kids would be there to see their momma on her game, regardless of what they heard. I would make their lies and accusations look weak by the time I was done, and that was on my soul.

Out of the 170 model submissions, I chose a cute vanilla-and-chocolate set, the two with the best chiseled bone structures for the angles, the slanted eyes I needed, and full brows to bring my vision to life. Prai and Foreign were so excited. They couldn't wait!

Prai said, "Girl, you know I lock up Saturday, so I can make sure I get them in and out and ready for Sunday. Foreign is goin' come get me to see the shoot, if that's OK?"

"Yes, friend, come through."

"Are you goin' have some snacks, or what are we doing for food?" He looked into his handheld mirror with one eyebrow raised.

"I'm goin' have a little spread. The boys will be there, so I'm goin' have something catered."

I scheduled the models to get their facials done the day before the shoot, which was advertising for Prai, which he appreciated. I didn't release the addresses to the locations until the consent forms were signed and returned. All our asses were in school still and in no position for lawsuits of any kind.

"It's the organization for me, sis." Prai laughed as I patiently waited on one model to return the signed documents. I was proud of myself. I thought, *Come through, Business Parys. Show up.*

When I arrived at the salon, Rachel walked me through the lockup process and the codes as she rushed out for her date. In between clients, I just sat in the front of the salon and flirted with Direct on FaceTime, accepting his invitation to our next link up.

As we said our goodbyes, a message from Prai came through. "Hey, girl, I need you to get to my job ASAP for a client. She need her lashes done."

"I got four more clients, and I'm there. Stall her as much as you can and let her know there is a travel and after-hour fee included in her service. I will let you know when I'm leaving here."

I started packing up equipment in between the clients I had to finish up for the evening. I cleaned up and packed the car, so once I finished that last client, I could lock up the salon and be on my way to Prai's job. I was fifteen minutes from the salon where he worked at part-time.

When I got there, I climbed the stairs and greeted

the owner. I small-talked with her as she showed me to the room where the client was. Opening the door, I saw it was Nicki Minaj! My mental thought was, *No fucking way!* But my face was poker. I smiled and shook her hand. Immediately, I set everything up. I was captured by her absolute beauty as she told me how she liked her lashes.

Nicki explained, "Prai showed me your IG page. Your work popping. I got a condo here, so if this works out, I will be back when I'm in town."

"You don't have to wait until you come to the city. If you need me, I'm open to travel." I wasn't missing a chance to be Nicki's go-to lash tech. I was taking advantage of the opportunity. Straight up, I would have been a fool if I didn't. I asked her if it was cool if I took a picture of us after the service for my page.

She replied, "We goin' do better than that." She hit the Live button on her phone. "Nicki in the building, in the A, getting my lashes slayed, for my pop out tonight." She plugged the salon we were in that her homegirl owned.

She showed me setting up, as I turned around in the video as often as possible to smile, throw up the peace sign, and pose with the cute pokey lip.

"She's so humble, y'all. Too cute. She was highly recommended. I'm going to keep y'all posted, but y'all already know if I like the work, it's a go. OK, barbs," she changed to her English accent, "talk to you soon."

Once she lay back on the table, I politely threw the back of her head and the cart with a quick Boomerang and saved it for a later post. I let her know I was doing it, but saving it. I couldn't be sneaky with Nicki.

"Girl, post your shit. You blessed. You in the presence of the queen. Run that up."

"Alright, now, thank you."

"Post that and hurry up. I gotta go."

"Say less."

I got to work. During the service, Nicki and her assistant talked as she approved her itinerary and double-checked her schedule. You know, business affairs. I just listened and took mental notes, visualizing how my life could be the same if I stayed focused with no disruptions. Once she got off that table, it was a blur. I could not believe I just serviced Nicki fucking Minaj. She looked in the mirror.

"Girl, you next up, lil' momma. That slant correct." She gathered her things together to leave, instructing her assistant to get my direct contact information. She leaned in to give me a hug. "You blessed, and don't you ever let no one else tell you different." She pointed them long-ass nails at me. "Now, when my assistant calls you, come through. Don't make me buy your ass out." She giggled, "You know I'm Nicki Minaj."

When she left, Prai came in to get the tea. We were hugging, laughing, and twerking all over the room. While the owner left with Nicki, we were alone to be silly for a minute. I hugged him so tight and thanked him for thinking of me. He didn't have to call me.

"Girl, that bullshit you went through on your job made it clear you got haters. I'm your friend. You just don't know it yet, and we goin' slay these dragons together. It ain't how you start. It's how you finish, and I'm looking at a rose that grew out of concrete. God told me to water you, baby."

I couldn't do anything but look at him while he spoke, holding back the tears with all my might. "You're amazing, Prai," I whispered as we started walking to the front of the salon. "What time Foreign coming to get you Sunday for the shoot, and what do you want me to get to eat?" I peeled off a $100 bill to give him a referral fee. It was the least I could do.

"You know I'm watching this figure, honey. I personally can go with some slutty vegan," he said sensually. We laughed, leaning into each other.

"Send me what you eat, and I will add it to what I ordered for the models and photographer. You ready for the models Saturday?"

"I scheduled them this morning—one for 6:30 and the other for 7:30."

"OK, cool. I will pay you Sunday, if that works? I

want to fuck up a check on the boys this weekend. I can't wait to see them."

When I got in the car to drive home, my energy was so light and fresh. My IG notifications let me know my page was lit! I moved the Boomerang from my Story to a post that was over 20k in likes, and the followers went up 5k. It was so overwhelming to the point that rolling a blunt was not even a thought. Those notifications motivated me to work out and eat a salad instead. I needed all of my mind and energy for my career because I just became an overnight success.

I stayed on my day-to-day routine until Friday. It was the day I was getting the boys. It was all I talked about in school that day. I was giddy. I had not seen my babies in a couple months. I had so much to tell them; I was ready to kiss them on their faces and call them young kings at least fifty times for no reason. I planned a slumber party for us with matching pajamas and all. All day, I cracked jokes, smiling so big my face hurt. All I could think about was seeing those two little brown boys of mine that evening.

I wasn't at my mom's house twenty minutes before Jared pulled up to drop off LaTrey. His hair wasn't cut, which wasn't a problem. It was something else for us to do. I immediately noticed his energy towards me was so off. He was uncomfortable hugging me when we greeted each other. I understood he had been hearing a lot of negative talk about me for the past couple months. I probably looked like I had a Medusa head on my shoulders. As I waited for Kingdom, I noticed Jared sitting in the car on the phone. The doorbell rang, and looking through the glass, I saw deputies at the door.

My mother yelled, "I know you ain't bringing this bullshit to my door! Your ass ain't been over here in months, and when you do come, you got the police here? This reminds me of that time the bounty hunter came for you after missing court when you were arrested for shoplifting at Macy's. Put this moment on your socials."

"I had no idea Keith was going to be this intentional." I walked to open the door.

One officer asked, "Are you Parys Germane?"

"Yes. How can I help you?"

"Can you sign right here?"

"What is this?"

"I'm serving you for child support abandonment."

At that moment, Kingdom walked up the porch steps with big eyes, wondering what was going on. My eyes immediately started watering as I signed the receipt of delivery and watched Jared pull off, knowing then he was waiting to see the show. My instant thought was, *This is some messy fuckboy shit.*

"Parys, what you got going on now, and why is it

at my door? You got your own place. Why didn't it come there? What if I had clients?"

"Do you think I had this scheduled to happen here today? Be serious. No, be supportive, caring, or loving. Why does it seem like you don't want to do that for me? Have my back. These really your friends? Why are you not checking your people about your family?"

"Oh, you can leave with the disrespect."

"No problem. You can't handle me being direct. You stay blessed, though."

"You on the north side now, thinking you are better than everyone else. You don't even talk the same. Everybody see it, bougie ass."

"You got that change I let you borrow for the phone bill."

"I can't believe you wouldn't want to help your mother in a time of need, only worrying about yourself. Just selfish."

"I figured you would go there. Come on my young kings." I walked out the door behind the boys. "I just wanted to see what you were goin' say, since you were saying everything else."

Quickly going into thought on how she used to get money out of me, asking me a couple of times in the past to sleep with exes to help her out of situations. If it wasn't for one of my exes helping her with a down payment to close, she would not have been in this property I was walking out of, while she had the nerve to slam the door behind me.

As soon as I got in the car, my vibe switched as the fog lifted. "Let's go to dinner somewhere. Where do you want to go?"

"Main Event."

"Let's go!"

Driving to Main Event, I craved a smoke break. I needed to mentally escape the bullshit from Jared, Keith, and my mom's lack of support. The only area of my life that was positive and gave me gratification was school and anything pertaining to work. I just wanted to stay in those spaces as much as I could. It was hard dealing with my reality. Work and school gave me a sense of safety, like a shield or a mental vacation. Shit, I was trying to stay in the space where I was celebrated, where I was able to pour into other women the healthy parts of me from the nurturing they were giving me.

I learned, as an aesthetician, I had to listen to my clients' problems sometimes, and they trusted what I said, knowing I came from a good space. It built a different kind of relationship between us, one that made them want to come back consistently for services. People didn't realize it, but it's more than a good service being offered. Those off-topic conversations were building bonds. I was feeding something in their soul that was hurt or confused just by sharing my opinions, while they were doing the same and they didn't even know it. To keep up with those conversations, it was essential for me to preserve my energy by welcoming positive interactions in my space. I couldn't afford to share my energy with those who were negative in my life. I had to be able to hear my inner voice clearly for the clientele base I was building.

We reached Main Event, and I wanted to load up my IG and FB Story. But my boys' hair wasn't cut, and I wasn't going to show them looking anything less than what I represented for myself. So I opted for Boomerangs, angles, distance, and low-light shots. I wanted everyone to know they were in the building with Momma, especially Direct, who wanted me to meet him that evening. I hated that I had to decline.

It had been a week-plus since we saw one another, but he texted me every morning and periodically during the day. We also talked late at night when he left events. I always answered his calls, no matter how late. He told me he wanted to hear my voice before he went to bed, which always made me smile.

Direct was definitely on my "he goin' get it" list. It was the random "thinking about you, stink" on his IG Story for me, tagged in his close friends. *There isn't anything quite like a man who publicly displays to the world that he cares or loves you. Yes, bae, let them know it's me.*

Once I loaded the Boomerang, Direct's comment came through first. "Oh, those my stepsons. I can't wait to meet them." This man even added my Story to his Story, with a caption, "my stepsons."

While the boys and I took a break from playing games to eat dinner, Kingdom asked, "Ma, you did Nicki Minaj's lashes?"

"I did! It was a dope moment."

LaTrey asked, "Were you nervous?"

"Yes and no. I have gotten confident in my skills. Your momma is that girl."

"Was she nice?" The boys alternated asking me questions, and I smiled at their curiosity.

"She was herself. I saw nothing fake, but it was my first time meeting her."

"You goin' do her lashes again?"

"I pray I do. Y'all know I'm doing this for y'all to see and experience a different life, right? I want y'all to do it better than me when it's your turn to step into your chosen paths. Be the king of whatever jungle you in. I don't give a fuck if it's selling dope. Be the kingpin." They both giggled.

Kingdom replied, "Momma, you so crazy."

"I'm being funny but serious too. Momma will love and support you regardless, no cap. Don't let anyone ever put shade on your shine. You are a product of me. Remember that when someone tries to dim your light. Always know they are reflecting their insecurities on you. Fuck them and everything they assume when it comes to you. Never forget these words. It's my responsibility to show y'all what I'm saying in real time so you don't forget. You will know who you are from and where you came from. Period." I paused to take a bite of food. "I have a photoshoot at the house Sunday for a lash brand that wants to work with me, so the apartment will be busy for a couple hours with models, a photographer, and a makeup artist."

LaTrey tilted his head. "Why don't you do the makeup?"

"I want to put my best into the brows and lashes, and I'm the creative director on the shoot. I didn't want to spread myself too thin, you know?" I needed this conversation and time with my boys. It felt so good being able to share my feelings with them. It felt safe. They were mine, so I could be honest and free to express myself. My two besties!

Kingdom stopped playing with his straw to ask, "You still got our new stuff at the new place?"

"Of course. Where else is it gonna be?" They knew everything I'd been posting since we separated, indicating to me that a lot of conversation was had in front of them. It then was confirmation to me that my boys' perspectives were targets, they were being groomed. The co-parents made sure they planted the seeds of hatred toward me so it continued, not generation to generation. They saw the direction I was headed as intimidation that I would surpass their endeavors, and even if I didn't, it poked at their personal insecurities I was in the position I was in.

I made so many mistakes as a young mother that I wished I could fix overnight, but I had to trust the process. My boys deserved to have a better mother, so I had to keep pushing through the growing pains. The urgency to correct myself to give them a better me was absolutely worth it. My boys were worth it for me. I had to realign the way I moved within myself. I was on that type of time.

The weekend continued and was completely peaceful. I took them for haircuts, bought them two outfits each, and went to throw the football in the park. I uploaded every move to my IG Story and created a mini "quality time" vlog. I was late showing social media all the shit I have ever done for them and the things we did together, but I was in my own mental block thinking it wasn't good enough, when I could have been showing the growth the whole time.

No lie, though, I never thought I'd see my life in its current state. I was really breathing a little. I always thought I'd be hustling and bustling forever. I was completely and totally focused on my present moment. *I'm not going backwards.*

When Sunday morning came, I had the highest level of energy I ever experienced, even higher than doing Nicki the previous week because I was directing this production. All I could think about was how it was going to add to my platform. The brand had over 500,000 followers. That kind of exposure would change my career, and I knew it.

I set the intentions of the house with good energy as I cleaned before I took the boys to church that morning. In service, I asked God for nothing but a positive union with every creative person that walked in the door that day. On the way home, we picked up the catered food orders for the shoot and went to the grocery store.

My only sadness stemmed from not wanting the boys to go back to their dads that evening after the shoot. But I did have a date that evening with Direct. *Momma gotta have a life too, Jodie.* I was looking forward to seeing him and what he had planned.

The boys helped me set everything up. They were just as excited as I was about the shoot, which was a joy to see. The day passed smoothly. I was beyond satisfied with everything from the photographer to the models to Foreign's makeup. It was a productive, soft-life Sunday, for sure.

Later, driving the boys to my mom's house, Kingdom asked, "Are we coming back over next weekend?"

"Do y'all want to?"

Both boys replied in sync, "Yes."

"I need y'all to stand up for me. I'm your mother. No one loves you or will love you as much as I do EVER." I turned to LaTrey. "I know you are still mad at me for that one boyfriend that hit you back in the day. Baby, Momma didn't know any better, but I do now. I'm sorry for not protecting you when I should have. I was wrong." To them both, I continued, "I'm sorry for leaving y'all at that stranger's house the evening in Miami to run in the streets, to go stripping in the club. I was wrong. Parents make mistakes, especially young parents, 'cause we are learning and growing up too. I picked up habits from how I was raised and perpetuated them. That was wrong. I have done nothing short of trying to be a better person for myself and y'all for some years now. Change doesn't happen overnight. It's a process. If y'all judge me, wait 'til I finish my process of change so you can take everything into consideration not just a phase. I'm working as fast as I can, learning as I go. I was fifteen and nineteen. Shit was such a blur to be real, and all I knew was I loved my boys when I didn't know love for myself, and sincerely, I knew I had to do whatever I could for y'all. From the time I knew I was pregnant with y'all, I knew I had to find purpose to keep developing into someone better, some way, somehow. Y'all became that motivation. Never doubt or let anyone else put doubt in your mind about it. Trust me. People know how much I love y'all 'cause I have done everything I knew to do to take care of y'all. Some people will never get that type of love from me, and they know it, so they are going be jealous of y'all." I thought about Jared and Keith, who came from very distant mothers. Their relationships with them were trash. Neither of them respected their moms for different reasons. Now, they were passing down their traumas to their children. It was my fault for not doing my homework, just living in the moment not paying attention to detail.

Dropping the boys off at my mom's, I felt it was in my best interest not to go in. I was dressed with a glam face. I had Foreign beat before she left; the day was going too good to ruin. I wasn't going in that lady's house for her to fuck up my vibe. I had a date. I was ready to be taken advantage of, honestly.

It was heartbreaking to watch them walk up those steps. I just hoped they were in a happy space. They each carried three bags full of new drip. They were ready to wear their new clothes. Their dads didn't buy them anything new after they went through the new things they were left with. LaTrey got hand-me-downs while watching his siblings get new things, and Kingdom said he was told he was waiting on a child support check. Such a psychological mind fuck. Yuck!

I called Direct to tell him I was on the way. I don't even think he let the phone ring twice before he answered it.

"Come to me, now, lovebug. You've been playing with me."

I laughed. "Boy, I'm on my way."

"No disrespect, leave that boy title away from me. I'm your fucking man."

"Not big dick energy? OK, then, Papi, I'm on my way."

"OK. I got a sprinter downstairs waiting on you, so let me know when you pull up."

My heart dropped. Butterflies danced in my stomach. I knew he was going to lay a doll down tonight, especially once I got out of the car in this dress. The body had been hydrated with distilled water seven days a week, yoga five days a week, Whole Foods organic fruit and vegetables four days this week, and wheatgrass shots three times a week. I was just simply pure and untainted.

I called to let him know I was outside. As he said, the sprinter was outside waiting on me when I pulled up.

"I see you. Look to your left, behind the door."

Why was this man standing there with two dozen of The Million Roses and trying to hold his phone on IG Live already? I couldn't do anything but smile as I backed my car in the visitor's parking spot in front of the building. He was such a showoff.

"Hey, y'all. I just wanted y'all to see her face when she pulled up and see what I got myself into for the evening." He walked over to open my door after struggling to set the flowers on the hood of the car. "Sneaky links, remove my number from your phone. I don't want you. Wifey home." He chuckled to himself.

"You too much," I said as he reached for my hand to help me out of the car. He kissed me on both cheeks, like he was French, before closing my car door.

"Worth the wait, little momma. You know I'm not playing with you."

"As you should not, capital and hard *T*."

Laughing, he replied, "You funny. We are on a schedule. You got everything you need right here. You know you are leaving from here to go to school in the morning, right?"

Looking puzzled, I said, "Uh, I didn't, but I—"

"I got you some clothes and shit upstairs. I'm not playing any games with you, Parys. I want to show you something different." He passed the flowers to the driver and helped me in the sprinter. "This fucking dress coming off, on my momma." He stared in detail at my body.

The sprinter was dressed with more roses. From what I could see, there were at least seven dozen total.

As we rode to the restaurant, Direct said, "Look, I ain't rich, but I ain't broke. I can get a favor from anyone in the city 'cause they really fuck with me. They know I'm up next with this comedy shit. I want someone by my side before I walk through the doors of success, so I know it's real. I been watching you grinding, crying, getting your dumb ass embarrassed by your baby daddies' wives, that lame-ass shit. Now you are doing celebrities, the big names. You know you are goin' places, right? Your nigga got to be a real boss to have your back, I'm going to support you. I want you to know you been motivating me to step my game up so I can complement what you got goin' on times ten."

I didn't even know he knew about the Facebook post from Adrienne. That let me know he was lurking. A little stalkerish, but it was cute. Still, I drifted off for a second, thinking, *Where is his car?*

"You know I could make a call on that drama. Shut that shit down. Ain't nobody gonna play with you when I'm with you. I'm not going."

"Calm down, crazy. They hate my growth. I really started from the bottom, but I'm here now."

"Where you belong."

"I agree. But at one point, I accepted to be treated less than my true worth, really not knowing who I was, before I discovered that wasn't the way to go. I have two court appearances, one for a civil suit for child support and child abandonment coming up."

"What the fuck!? Parys, what kind of niggas you was fucking on?" he asked, laughing. "They are doing some other type of shit, ain't they."

"Getting in my bag and they're mad. That's all. They are using the moment to express pain and hurt from years ago, using the boys as a strategy to get their lick back from whatever they were mad at me about."

"Didn't you just take the boys shopping and spend time? They are on bullshit. They should want to see their baby momma's doing better. Their wife ain't on your side?"

I looked at him with a side eye and a pouty lip.

"Oh, you're a fine baby momma. They can't handle it, damn. Baby, I'm here now." He grabbed my hand with a firm grip and deep stare.

I had been on some nice dates before, but this was definitely top three. From the looks of things, the restaurant was reserved just for us. We were in a private booth, and I couldn't see anyone else in our area. The night ended as expected, with my legs in the air, moaning his name, agreeing with every word he whispered in my ear as I was surrounded in his place with several dozen roses. I loved him. Yes, in almost one month and a second date, I was in love.

Waking up the next morning, I got dressed and

headed to school. The fact that Direct had the right size in the Alo Yoga 'fits he got for me to wear under my smock was mind-blowing. He listened and took detailed notes in the conversations we had. I didn't realize his questions about my clothing and shoe size were related to the fact that he was building me a section in his closet.

As soon as I settled in class, still floating on a cloud, Rachel called me. I quickly walked into the hall to answer it.

She jumped right in. "I have an emergency. Can you cover my appointments today?"

"Starting at what time?"

"The next hour."

"Let me try to move some things around here at school and call you in twenty minutes." I wondered if Prai or Foreign could swipe my card for me. We had to swipe our own time cards or receive disciplinary actions if caught doing it for another student. It was viewed as stealing clocked hours.

I approached Prai and Foreign. "It's an emergency at the salon. Rachel needs me to cover for her appointments. Can you clock me out?"

Prai looked away from his handheld mirror. "Go make that money. Baby, I got you." He reached out for my time card.

Foreign added, "And I can be a distraction." Our instructor stood by the time card machine.

I didn't hesitate. I returned Rachel's call, giving her the green light, and stopped at Whole Foods to stock up on food for the day. I knew I wouldn't have time to run out on my first day opening and closing the salon.

I remembered how my mom worked from open to close. I knew what to expect. And as expected, I was mentally exhausted by the end of the day. Rachel never called to check on me with her clients, which indirectly told me she was secure. And, it was cool. I did not have one complaint all day.

Communication was key, and once I explained to the clients that Rachel had an emergency and asked that I service her clients, they understood. Some mentioned that they followed me on social media, which was refreshing to know. One even said she told Rachel to run her social media up. Rachel did try but wasn't too successful. I couldn't judge her by her social media status, not having the solid clientele base she had, so I just listened and made a mental note.

Once I finished the day, I needed a reset. Damn, how these tables had turned while I sent a Cash App to Prai out of appreciation. Prai was going to stay in my pocket. He showed up for me every time I needed him. He was a team player, and I felt that Rachel would need me again someday.

I wanted her to know she had someone she could rely on. From what her clients told me, Rachel had been in business for five years without a vacation. She needed a break. The clients mentioned other techs were in there before, but they never worked out. The clients never accepted their work, whereas mine was complementary to Rachel's.

Waking up the next morning, I was tired as hell. It quickly helped me understand that I didn't want that feeling for an extended period of time. I needed more brand endorsements and a product to sell. I became obsessed with creating different styles of lashes to complement the client's natural eye shape, not the cookie-cutter style everyone else did.

While I was responding to Nicki's assistant, asking to service her in a couple days. Maybe if I made one for Nicki in particular, she could help me get it off the ground? I thought about her style, her look, and her brand. I immediately started drawing designs and thinking I need to buy some products and materials to inspire me to move on this thought.

During the next couple days of in my routine all I could think about was how standing up all day from open to close was going to get dead real fast. I wanted to work smart, not hard. My newfound dreams and aspirations quickly started interfering with my focus at school. I wanted these classes done. I had what I needed from this school venture. The clients in my contacts were up to a consistent forty-five from school alone, even though my initial goal was 100. In my opinion, I was doing good turning tips to profit.

Just when I forgot about Jamaica, she called, talking about how shit slowed up for a sec but we were back on. This time, I needed to be in Arizona for four days. The money from the run would take care of a lot, enough to put a pause on the streets. I wasn't letting the risk of trafficking interfere with a solid future in my career.

If I grind this out for the next two years, I could carry this industry. It would work for me, instead of the other way around. From my grandma to my mom, I saw how drained they were pushing through their journey in this industry. It was good to see hard working women, but they stayed that way and never really leveraged enough to retire out of the industry. My grandma worked behind the chair until she died. I didn't want that for myself, and my mom was headed down that same path. Nah, I was good on that even from the thought.

My mom had products, but they were never positioned to work for her. They were just additional income, like a hustle that made good money. From what I saw, she didn't really capitalize on the opportunity—no advertising, just relying on the word-of-mouth advertisement.

While that's cool, it's not enough for this industry. The reflective thoughts using those examples helped me piece this puzzle together of what I could do differently. I needed to focus on getting this lump sum, which caused a serious pickle. I needed to be on the road to Arizona, in school, and at the salon. Going on the road put me up where I needed to be financially, so I needed that check, and after doing my research, I needed to invest in the patent and production of a sample lash style once it was done.

Time management was vital. I couldn't take that many days off from school and couldn't be away from the salon that long, but I had to figure out how to make it work. As I dressed for school, I remembered Nicki's appointment was also that day. I made sure I packed my measurement pouch to take her eye measurements for my design. I spent the entire day mentally planning, thinking about the money I would make, what I needed to take care of with the money, Direct, the salon, and finishing this damn program. It was all just a mental fog. I was glad to end once I finished with Nicki later that day. Nicki was a pleasure to service yet again. I posted her to my page. It was such a sign of respect to my service that she continued to patronize my business.

Direct was on my ass about coming to his place and leaving from there to go to school since I hadn't been there. *Sir, I'm trying to stay home and make my plans, but you know my man got to be happy.* He was the only person I was really worried about while being gone for four days. He asked so many consecutive questions, and I would be coming up with too many lies to keep up. This was one thing about my life I knew and was glad he wasn't aware of. It was something I couldn't fathom to share… *"Hey, babe, I traffic periodically." How crazy does that sound sharing?* We had not crossed the topic, and I didn't volunteer the information.

Honestly, I didn't mind him not knowing. He knew too much already. It was cool that he wanted to know things about me, but there were things I wasn't ready to share. I didn't want anything to be used against me at a later date. Was I wrong for that? It was a fact that he had not shown me he was that type, but in my past relationships, people used what they knew about me as their "one up" to manipulate me for what they wanted. I guess I was just being cautious and taking my time, but our relationship was moving so fast. With social media involved, it wasn't helpful.

I was labeled as his lady. He had us doing a couple skits and wearing matching outfits. If you could only imagine the look I had on the side of my brain, listening to him explain his new idea for our next skit while we ate dinner at his place that night. I liked him—correction, loved him—but I had everything else going on in my mind. He was obsessed with me, so I went along with whatever he was on. It hurt me to feed him some bullshit, but I had too much to do.

"Bae, I was booked for a job in Arizona, so I will be out of town for a couple days," I said as I showed him an example of an inquiry I was reading over.

"How long is a couple days? You want me to come? We can make it a vacation. Oh, I got a skit we can do that would go up in views. I'm waiting on YouTube to respond to me for us too."

"Bae, I wish. I'm taking an advancement class and working at two sites. I did an ad to start a pop-up salon service to businesses and got a request from one there."

"Damn, lil' momma." He walked over to pick me up, kissing me all over my face. "You thinking outside the box. They paying for your travel and hotel, right? You won't have time to play. I want you to focus. I'm gonna miss you. I can send you with whatever you need. If you need anything, let me know. I love you."

"I love you too." I thought, *Parys, you ain't worth shit for making up a partial lie to a nigga that is really investing his time in you.* Now, I did the ad for the businesses for the surrounding area for Atlanta, Georgia, but not Arizona. True, I just changed the state. No real harm done, right? I couldn't tell Direct what I was really doing. He would have started worrying and trying to shut my plans down, and that was an mmm-mmm!

I lined this schedule up, and I needed him not to be worried about me. Now Direct didn't have a car, but he moved around when needed and never asked me to use my car or take him anywhere. From what I saw, he had himself together. He was focused on the goals he wanted to reach.

We were a progressing power couple, which was the main reason why I started coming out of my comfort zone doing skits with him to publicly display to him the depth of our connection. Initially, I hesitated because of my insecurities and reluctance to experience a man who wanted to show everyone that I was loved and adored. I deserved what he showed me, and I needed to know that. I was appreciative of him because I saw a future with him. I just had not verbally expressed it, only showing him in the responses toward him.

When he called, I answered. When he texted, I texted back. When he wanted to see me, I made my way to him. I responded to him in every way. I didn't text-delay him or make him wait for a response to stroke my ego. I gave him no toxic actions. But that lie? I just gave him that. I wasn't perfect.

Now that Direct was in position, my next move was Jamaica. I needed her to move that run to the last two days of the week, allowing me to miss two days of school and the salon. I could block my weekend off at Rachel's, which was just a Saturday. It just made sense to move around in Arizona from Thursday to Sunday, getting back into my routine Monday like nothing happened. That needed to be the plan.

Chapter Six

I had a week to get my schedule together for Rachel. Requesting the days I needed off, she asked me more questions than I thought she needed to or I was willing to share. I professionally let her know I needed the time for personal reasons, and that was as far as I went.

Rachel had called off again since the last time. She was getting real comfortable with asking me to cover for her, keeping me overbooked. I was down to the last sixty days in the program before graduation, and it looked and smelled like I needed my own space. I finalized my plans to use the money from the Arizona run to open my salon suite and invest in the patent for the lash I finally finished for Nicki that was the next-level style for the lash game.

My court dates took place before I traveled, so at least that business would be handled. Thankfully, I wouldn't have any surprises coming back. The courts wanted me to submit my tax information or a recent check stub to calculate the child support amount and any receipts from payments already paid. The court dates were two days apart in different counties. I was ready to get the shit over with, knowing how mentally draining these days would be.

The first court day was with Jared. Looking over the documents, I was still appalled that Adrienne's name was on everything before his. What kind of foolishness was that? My check stubs from Arch Me were strong enough to verify the income to validate payments ordered, so I wasn't worried about the payments increasing.

I represented myself in the case. I was not investing my hard-earned money on nothing pertaining to the subject of getting a lawyer. Knowing these circus-clown-ass folks were on complete bullshit, stretching the situation thin, showing they weren't busy with their lives. Something was missing from their lives because I couldn't understand how they had the time and so much focus on me. I never thought to put this amount of energy into Jared and Keith's cases when they were on child support. I never bothered to follow up with the modification review or anything 'cause I was busy with my life and affairs. It was time away from whatever hustle I was on at that time.

On the day of the hearing, they showed up with

lawyers as we stood in front of the judge. What I didn't expect was for Adrienne to pull out my social media clips. Their lawyer asked that the emergency financial increase to the current support order be based on the average celebrity makeup artist salary, asking for an additional $275. The judge granted that since my employment changed before the three-year modification period.

Given that I didn't have legal knowledge or the correct terminology to represent myself, I sat there overwhelmed, looking like a complete idiot. I was so frustrated with everything that I accepted the ruling with no fight. The payment was calculated at over $1,000, and I hadn't gotten to Kingdom's court date yet, which was now less than forty-eight hours away.

At my second court appearance for Kingdom, the day felt like a repeat. The only difference was that Keith himself led the conversation with their lawyers. He adopted Adrienne's tactic of using my social media against me and spoke up more than Jared did in his case. The calculation was almost the same as LaTrey's payment.

I shared with the judge that I was just placed on child support for my other son, thinking it would help reduce the payment, but it made me look irresponsible instead.

I just folded in my skin when the judge said, "Ma'am, you have another open case for child support?"

Leaving the hearing, I could only think that I was paying three times more than Jared and Keith paid me, or were supposed to anyway.

Later that night, I was catching Direct up to speed about my court appearances after not seeing him in a couple days. He just quietly listened. I could tell by the look in his eyes how disappointed he was that I was going through the extra bullshit, knowing it came from a place of jealousy and hate. It felt good to have someone to just listen, rub my feet, and tell me they were there for me however I needed.

This man was really pulling at my heartstrings, playing a song that was so healthy. I thanked God for having someone to talk to and love me at a time when I really needed it. That evening, we did five skits so he could load them up while I was in Arizona for those four days. Our other skits went up on his pages like crazy, from what he told me, so he needed more to keep them consistent.

Jamaica partnered me with another driver, and we had a strategic schedule to follow to get us back in town by the end of the weekend. We arrived in Arizona the next day. First thing, I called Direct, to cover up the flight schedule I lied about only being able to text him the first day. I explained I had to adjust to the time difference, organize everything with the point of contact, edit pictures with the photographer from the brand shoot, and make sure I was clocked in at school with Prai. Yes, it was a little truth and lie, but I was busy that first day. He was cool, only focusing on the numbers from his social media pages from our skits. Me being on his pages in skits was new for his platform, so the responses were important to him.

In the down time between loading up and our departure, I hiked up the South Phoenix mountain to meditate, thinking about everything I wanted to put in place when I returned home. My child support was now the same as my rent and car insurance. I wanted to upgrade my car, but I didn't see that happening until I achieved my first set of goals, factoring everything into consideration. I wanted to stay within my budget given what I would make from this trip. I had to think about my patent investment, the boys, and the expenses of everyday living.

In the time of my travels, I wasn't posting anything personal about my life. I only uploaded the paid sponsor posts, business content I'd stored in my phone, servicing Nicki recaps, and the brand work once the edits were complete. I had enough content for at least a week or so. I had to post every day to stay in the algorithm.

Everything was in place on the East Coast for us to return home when Adrienne called my phone.

"When is your first payment due?"

"Girl, you got to be drunk. Why are you on my phone?"

"I'm trying to schedule my hair appointment."

"Don't call my phone unless it's about LaTrey." I hung up.

I was glad I was so far away. She was provoking me. I knew she wanted me to fight her so she could press charges and try to damage my reputation. Her call made me the quietest I had ever been, just collecting my thoughts, trying to keep the energy light for what we were doing. Adriene's call was a distraction, and I was happy I could see through it, instead of responding as ignorantly as I wanted to.

I blocked the house number. I was only accepting calls from either Jared's cell or her cell moving forward, and she wasn't bold enough to call me from her cell number. I slapped her so many times in my mind for at least an hour. Adriene moved to the realm of "on sight" when I saw her, and I hadn't been in that head space in a minute.

I took some time to make sure I prayed and redirected my energy, only seeing myself home in Atlanta. This trip was my last and biggest. I needed nothing but focus. I had too much at risk to entertain her. I thought about keeping the money coming in from these little trips several times while I was driving back to Atlanta, but the risk was too much. Already sitting on $10,000 en route to pick up another $10,000 made it so tempting to consider.

Returning to Atlanta was a relief. I wasn't even in the city for two hours before I was called to see Bae. Regardless of exhaustion, you know I went. We were so glad to see each other. I missed him, but he bombarded me with so many questions. He wanted to know why I didn't post any pictures from the class on my Stories or at least any pictures of the clients. I used the excuse that I didn't want it to be held against me in court. "I didn't want to show too much."

The man asked to see my phone, to look through my pictures, before I shut the attack down. I asked him, "Why you not trusting me all of a sudden?"

"I don't like you traveling like that without me. You were gone too long. We are a couple now publicly. We have to be together more. Our YouTube views are running up, getting a lot of traction, and monetizing. We have to be in sync."

"Babe, OK, but I have too much goin' on to add cheating to my schedule. So don't come for me like that, please. That ain't it. It's us, you know that. I'm investing in the patent of the lash I created for Nicki, and I want my own salon suite. That's the focus for me."

"Once you get everything as you want it, I want you to work with me. I want you to myself as much as possible. I want you to work without labor. It's easier ways to make money, Parys, but fulfill your dreams first. Get it out the way."

"OK, Papi. Get it out the way. Let's address that for later, but you realize I haven't been in love in a minute. You are different from anyone I have dated in the past. I'm not used to the public attention, so it's an adjustment for me. It's not you. Papi. Everyone know I'm yours. You have me on a post every chance you get. We stay on the phone, I text back, and when you call me to get here, I'm here just like now, and I just got back in town."

"It's got to be that way. I just want us to be in sync, showing unity. We growing together. It looks positive for the community we building. Don't play with me 'cause I'm not playing with you. I be on my player shit. Everybody know I don't do relationships. Shit, I'm usually fucking on these hos and leaving. You got a drawer full of panties, bras, PJs, and workout clothes, and I made more space in the closet for you. That ain't for no reason, Parys. Oh, yeah! I got you those new Js and a pair of Dior slides when I got me some things Saturday and a few outfits. We need to go outside and take some pictures soon." He quickly transitioned his energy to a lighter conversation.

I ran into his room to see the new drip, stopping midway. "But wait. We building a community? Let's table that for later." I realized I had not done an update on Direct's pages to see where the numbers were in a minute. "Papi, let me see what you brought me. You didn't even tell me." I opened the boxes, thinking I should do an unboxing haul video.

Direct walked behind me on Live. "My lady spoiled. I don't play with her. Try them on, stink."

"Bae, OK. Let me add it to my stories real quick." I hadn't posted a "flex on 'em" in a week. My child support had already increased. I might as well.

Getting back into the routine of the school schedule was an adjustment the next morning. I was so ready to see my Prai. We texted and spoke a couple times while I was traveling. He was so happy I made it back home. I could tell from the hug he gave me. It was so tight. He really knew the truth about the trip and was on standby just in case I needed him to bond me out.

While in school, I contacted the patent company to submit the research application. I started looking into salon suites as well, as the dialogue between Rachel and me was a little off. I inquired about my contract before I left, and her initial response was shady. I asked her to move me from commission to booth rent once I graduated, knowing I was bringing my platform and clients with me working in the salon full-time.

I knew staying in a commission-based contract would give me more control over my money, bills, and the investment endeavors. I also didn't want my personal affairs to be a conversation piece at no point while I was working. I knew it was going to be a problem when she texted me while I was on the road, asking if my boyfriend could help me. I thought, *Ma'am, that's my personal business, and you watching me too much on IG for you to even ask me that question.*

I responded quickly, "Help me with what?"

"With your personal affairs."

"If he was or wasn't, how are you comfortable enough to ask me the business that I don't share with you?"

"I see he really likes buying you things."

"Oh, Rachel, since we are on personal time, mind your business, ma'am. You are completely out of pocket."

"I didn't mean to offend you."

"Then don't."

The moment further motivated me to find my own

space. Direct couldn't believe his eyes when he read the messages.

He said, "I like how you checked her ass. She was trying to get in your business to get in your business, you know?"

"I know."

Direct gave me money for all types of things, and I shared that with no one. It wasn't their business. I covered only my utilities, and he paid the rent at my apartment that I was barely in, along with whatever else he wanted. Direct didn't want me stressing over money and paying too many bills as he thought it took away focus from my craft and building my clientele while I was in school. I loved that about him he was always looking for a way to relieve me from what he considered may be stress on me.

I wasn't looking forward to seeing Rachel when I went back to work, but I had to keep moving forward. Even if I had a funny feeling there would be tension in the salon.

As I thought it, Rachel texted me. "I have a doctor's appointment this afternoon. I won't be here when you return today, but the schedule is booked, if you are able to take care of my clients."

"I wish I would have known that. I booked a lot before I left and have been booking since I've been away. So that's my schedule and yours once again. Were you considering my schedule?"

"Oh, I didn't know."

"You didn't ask either. Let's schedule a meeting to really talk."

"Let's do dinner tomorrow night, like 7 p.m. Does that work for you?"

"Yes, that's cool."

I didn't have anything else to say. I had to wrap my mind around being overbooked all day. Sharing the news with Direct, he let me know he would meet me at the salon to entertain the crowd while I worked to help things flow better.

"Women loved a man in their presence with positive energy, especially one who can make them laugh, so it would be a good distraction if you ran a little behind on the schedule."

Direct added, "I'm goin' make sure I get you a salad. You want one from Whole Foods or Fresh to Order? That way you can just go straight there."

"The usual is fine. Can you get me a shot of wheat-grass too?"

"I'm goin' take you to dinner tonight, and we outside. It's Magic City Monday. I want to meet some of the guys there, and you need a break."

"OK, Papi."

I thought to myself, *Sir, I'm going to be tired.* I

wanted to tell him I didn't want to go out because I would likely be drained from the clients, but I didn't, being appreciative that he wanted to make my day easier however he could. It was the consideration for me, just heartthrob energy!

Direct came through and helped me get through the day, as he said he would. The day was busy and entertaining. He definitely helped those six hours seem like three. He went Live for at least an hour, which helped me gain more followers, plugging me the whole time with shoutouts. Direct showed the work I put in from the clients who were open to being seen on his Live. It was a great advertisement. He came in the room where I worked when I was between clients every chance he got to kiss me and tell me how proud he was. I think it turned him on to see me servicing beautiful, professional women back to back.

"Girl, I will do anything for you, deadass. You working so hard."

If I could have had one moment to give him a little fellatio, I would have. His support that day was top tier. He deserved it. It was so convenient that he lived so close to the salon because once I was done, we went to change clothes for dinner and go to Magic City. Surprisingly, I wasn't as tired as I expected.

At dinner, Rachel texted, "You had the clients on your man's Live today?"

I showed her message to Direct, and he said, "Don't respond to her. You off work. She ain't check the shit, then. She shouldn't be trying to check the shit now. Your page went up today, and she mad. Matter of fact, let me see the phone." I started noticing Direct had a temper when it came to me. It was one thing to hear about someone bothering me when he wasn't around. If he was there, he would say something for sure.

Direct asked, "Y'all got dinner tomorrow night or whenever, right?"

"Yes, Papi." I kept breaking up my halibut.

He took my phone and replied to Rachel's text himself. "We will talk tomorrow." He then turned back to me. "Let her wait for an explanation until then. We up from here. Nothing and no one interfering with what we got goin' on. I'm still trying to figure out what I want to do to your baby daddies. I just ain't spoke on it." He stared deeply into my eyes.

"OK, baby. Don't lose your appetite or make me lose mine. Thank you for handling that. I hear what you are saying, and I agree with you." I paid for dinner that night, showing a little reciprocity toward him. He grabbed me from the back, walking out the door wide-legged, in complete pride on his IG Live.

"See, y'all got to get yourselves one of these. My queen! We are on the way to turn up at Magic tonight. Pop out. Turn up with us."

I thought he was only saying that, knowing we were in a section with complimentary bottles all night. The night was a movie per usual for Magic City Monday.

Between work, the club, and servicing Papi, I didn't get to sleep until 5 a.m., and school started at 7:30. I walked into class with a mismatched-colored yoga set from something I grabbed in the dark, not wanting to turn the light on, and some dark Chanel shades. I felt like I was about to vomit at any given moment. I didn't even remember being on my IG Story that hard until Prai and Foreign told me. They laughed, asking if I needed a double espresso latte, hot or cold.

I responded, "Baby, I need some more sleep, and I got to deal with Rachel this evening after work. I got to get my shit together." I knew I wouldn't sober up until the afternoon. I was definitely taking a nap for lunch. I swore I could taste the seat, leaning back in my car for the rest I needed.

After my mandatory nap, I sobered up completely in enough time to walk into the salon for Rachel to fuss at me about the trash in the kitchen.

"While you were on social media and playing all day, you forgot to take the trash out. When I walked in, the entire salon smelled."

"Ma'am, I was doubled booked all day. Did you check the numbers from yesterday 'cause I'm sure they were up. Damn that trash if I forgot it. I was thrown off guard, not knowing you put your afternoon schedule on me. Come at me better 'cause it's not the best day for simple bullshit. No bullshit, actually." I set my Valentino crossbody on the desk and looked at her like I was ready to slap intelligence into her.

"The numbers were really good."

"I juggled your clients and mine and didn't miss a beat. The first thing I'm expecting to hear is that I did a good job, not questions about the trash. What the fuck?"

"OK, calm down. You right. You know that's a peeve of mine, and my client was here. It was a little embarrassing."

"Embarrassed. You know what? I'm not available for dinner tonight. I'm not sitting at no table across from you feeling like I do." I looked at her schedule. "We goin' talk between 5:15 and 5:30 'cause it won't take long." Rachel had called my stupid for the day, so I answered, giving her no time to respond as my client walked in the door.

"Oh, that's what we are doing?"

"YES!" My eyes bulged even bigger. If she said one more thing, I was walking out and showing out on the way.

A couple hours later, I dove into our talk first. I was on her ass. She asked for it.

I said, "I'm finishing school in a month. I want to

revisit my contract. I want it changed to booth rent, with a weekly or monthly payout—your choice. I want to start out with six months and revisit from there every six months."

"I don't think you have enough experience to do booth rent. I'm willing to keep you on the same commission, revisiting negotiation sixty days after you graduate. I have been taking a chance having you in here without your license this entire time."

"Well, well, well. Isn't that something convenient to use. Were you thinking about those chances when you left me to open and close? You are choosing to use things how you see fit, and for that, I'm going to turn in my two weeks' notice tonight, out of pure professionalism."

I walked back to my room to prepare for my next client. Afterward, I did just as I told Rachel and emailed her the notice before I walked out that day, with the trash in hand.

I was so glad I listened to my intuition and looked for the new space. I received a response from one location five miles from the salon, which was perfect as I was under a competition clause that prevented me from opening a location within three miles.

After speaking to Rachel, I could tell she was taken back from my hasty response. I had to make an immediate decision because she was quickly becoming another problem I didn't need. Thinking about how my talents had grown, I knew I didn't have time for Rachel's distractions.

When I saw Direct later, he was so proud of me for making a solid decision by trusting my gut and moving on my intuition immediately, instead of second-guessing myself.

"I'm nervous, but I feel like I had to do something. Rachel called my stupid today. I really almost cussed her out. I don't know if it was the hangover or the situation." We laughed together over memories from the night before.

"No, be that boss lady, Parys. You checked her professionally. You are going to be just fine. We have a couple social media platforms, which means free marketing and advertising. You can't lose. Do you want to throw a party or a dinner for your graduation? It's a couple weeks away from now. I need to make my plans."

"I really don't know how to answer that question. I never had anyone want to plan something for me, to be honest."

"Wait. Didn't you graduate from another trade some years back? You didn't have a party or dinner with your family and friends to celebrate?"

"No, I didn't. To answer your question and yes I did get a trade before this one. I guess once I dropped out of high school and got my GED a couple years after. It was always get it done and move to the next goal for me. You have to remember, babe, I was a teenage mom, and my family held me to that."

"It wasn't a death sentence or a reason to just box you in to that title. You were trying to better yourself along the way. I mean, even if you was fucking up from time to time, your graduations of any kind deserve to be celebrated. It encourages the person. Shit, it's motivating."

"At least one would think it's supposed to be that way. Look, babe, I'm not trying to create a symphony concert, but when I got baptized last year, I invited my mom and younger sister. They didn't show. I was there alone. After that experience, I was done with celebrating myself. I accepted that my family wasn't comfortable with supporting me, and it was cool."

"Well, I'm here to tell you it ain't cool. That shit toxic and damaging as fuck. No one really knows this, but my parents ain't my biological parents. My biological parents died when I was seven. My dad committed suicide from depression 'cause he was feeding my mom dope that she overdosed from, so I was in foster care 'til I was seventeen. The last ten years, I was able to get some family dynamic structure to know how shit goes a little, and what you experienced ain't it! You deserve to be celebrated. You are doing amazing, putting your life together, and everyone sees it, Parys, know that some just don't want to. They have whatever narrative they've been rehearsing for so long. It's just hard for them to break. It's not all you. It's them not feeling comfortable in reciting the new version of the narrative, and to be honest, they can't keep up 'cause your shit keeps changing and getting better. They don't want to look wrong or like liars so they stick to the script, you know?"

Tears filled my eyes. "Thank you for sharing your feelings with me and trusting me with knowing about your parents and how you were raised. I haven't been able to be this transparent with a partner. It feels good, Direct. This, us, feels good."

"Parys, you need unconditional love, like for real, a love that doesn't want nothing from you in return, not any of that manipulation shit. It's like you only got temporary love if you were doing something and being a certain way for them to give it to you. You need a love that's goin' to understand that you come from a damaged place and not judge or hold that shit over your head. You just need a consistent groomer so you know that you are safe and you can be comfortable to be you without prejudice. They treat you like they do 'cause they don't want you to heal, but YOU will heal and be the amazing woman you deserve to be, especially if you put in the work. Fuck that, you hear me? I'm never leaving you for no one, no rumor, nothing in your past, NOTHING, girl. We goin' focus on these goals, accomplish them, and run this money the fuck up together."

"I want you to help me with the salon suite for my graduation gift."

"That's it? You don't want a vacation and a Chanel bag?"

"You just said you want us to run the money up, right? Let's stack hard for a year, like cutting the miscellaneous spending out at least 40 percent. I know it's shit we have to do to keep the community entertained and motivated, but let's tap in with a little priority and responsibility for us on a private level."

"I'm with that. How much longer do you have on your lease? You are not renewing it. That cuts out $1,400 I've been covering for the past three months. How much is your child support?"

"Collectively, $2,150."

"You know that ain't it, right?"

I answered in a shameful tone, "Yes, I do. They were only ordered to pay me $150-250 each when they were on child support, and they were in arrears when I took them off. Shit is crazy in my mind every time I think about it."

"Parys, my baby, spare me the details before I have someone run in their house tonight, ok?"

We continued to plan and agreed to a financial budget. I could only get this flexing ass, rising Internet sensation, to agree to commit for six months of saving. I was convinced our conversation from that day helped our relationship sink deeper. It was so obvious in our interaction with each other, in anything we did. It even showed in our skits as our engagement increased 27 percent within weeks. Life got so heavy. It felt like we were running through weeks within days. Before I knew it, graduation was upon me!

I was more excited than I expected, with a sense of mental relief, as school had become a hindrance in my schedule. Still, I was happy with what I accomplished and really proud of myself that I finished something else I started. I shared the celebratory moment with Direct and my peers.

I extended an invitation to my mom, but she politely declined. She said she was working, in a dry-ass tone. I accepted the fact that she was not available for any type of celebratory time. She just was not that type of person. If I was not involved in some upheaval that she could gossip about, she was just not interested.

I still posted the moment because, if nothing else, she watched what I was doing from my socials. Direct took me to dinner and bought me the waist-belt bag I wanted from Saint Laurent, so I was satisfied with the day. The salon budget wasn't completely tallied up, and we were working our plan. Like I told Direct that night at dinner, "The quicker I can get the salon finished, staying on schedule, the quicker I can scale it to six figures in ninety to 120 days. I know I can and will make a million within two years, and that will be beautiful for my lineage. I just wanted to set an example for my family and hope it would result in similar successful outcomes for them in the future. Maybe I have to be the one to turn the page first."

After graduation, everything just sped up. I locked myself in a location for the salon suite. I negotiated the first three months' free rent due to the work that had to be done in the space. It was more of an investment than we initially calculated, due to the business license and passing the inspection.

I only saw the boys once since the new child support order was granted. I paid what I felt like paying on the new order amount, talking with the boys on our brief calls they shared things that I knew made me feel like they were being mistreated. Every time I spoke to them, as their mom, I could hear the discomfort in their voices. The co-parents were taking my little young kings through some financial and mental abuse releasing frustration from how they felt about me. Watching my social media didn't help from doing skits with Direct, to my graduation, to my work at the new salon, and servicing Nicki, so when the boys would describe their scenes of being outcasts within the households, I understood.

They told me they'd been ignored, verbally and mentally abused by their stepmoms, and even physically abused, as LaTrey spoke about a black eye from his dad. It was knocking on my "fuck them" door, and honestly, it didn't help that I thought about Adrienne getting her hair done with my money from her call when I was Arizona. I gave just enough child support to not miss a month, deciding that's how that was going to go for a while. I was not going to stop posting, doing skits, or whatever else I had going on because it was helping build our brands. I knew I was sacrificing my boys, but what was I supposed to do?

I tried to convince Direct that it might be too much. But the platforms were growing, and we knew the co-parents were watching. I said, "Maybe we should block them."

"Loveface, NO! They not goin' do anything but watch from another page. They paid for front-row seats. Give the people what they paid for."

We really had a heated debate about it. I even tried to threaten him. I told him to take me off his page or block them. I couldn't help but think about how it affected the boys.

He replied, "They see you making money on the Internet, and they mad."

"But I don't feel comfortable, need, or like no one counting my money. I'm not trying to impress my past."

Direct walked over to me and gave me a hug with a gentle rock as I cried in frustration. "Baby, I'm not changing shit about what we doing. You just have to accept that your past is goin' to watch you be successful. That's their karma, and don't feel bad for them. I'm sorry if this is uncomfortable for you, but I'm goin' through it with you. It's scary for me, but this is what we have to do to be leaders. We are that couple that people like to see. It gives them a chance to see that black love is possible. This is our life, Parys, and it's goin' keep getting bigger and better." He kissed me on my forehead. "Before you know it, they will be so far on the periphery, you won't see them anymore, and the boys will be home to enjoy your successes with you, with us. We have to come at this as a team, learning and trusting one another throughout the process, or it's goin' fall apart. Once we get used to it, it will get easier. I promise. We can't stop nothing, though, and I'm not sorry about that." He stopped rocking.

The last couple days at Arch Me with Rachel were intense, adding more stress with everything else going on in my mind. It seemed as if this lady pushed every patience button I had to get a negative reaction out of me. She was asking me,

"Did you ring up your last ticket?" looking over the tickets at the front desk.

"Yes. The total didn't add up right?"

"It was right."

"Then why did you ask me that?" I walked back in my space, closing my door behind me. I let every client I serviced know I would no longer be at the salon and directed them to my IG after I added a booking link to my profile. I didn't realize I had worked at Rachel's for almost six months. I had grown so much during the time. I learned so much about my capabilities, my independence, and my craft. My confidence radiated a warm feeling in my soul that expelled through the roof, just thinking of what else I was able to produce creatively after moving on from Rachel's.

On my last day, I let Rachel know I appreciated her for the opportunity. She was an amazing talent, and her tenacity and stability were admirable. Rachel's established longevity was something I wanted to have for my business, so I planned to mimic what she did in order to get it. I knew the transition into my own salon required me to apply every note I had taken from my experiences from working with my mom and Rachel for me to see the foundation of the success I was seeking.

My salon wasn't quite ready to open yet. We gave ourselves six weeks after leaving Rachel's, so I offered both mobile services and opened up my home, work-ing out of the living room. The space needed a sink installed, which required plumbing, re-tiling the floor on the service side, carpeting on the waiting side, a tele-vision with surround-sound speakers, and repainting of the entire 600-square-foot suite. It was located on the third floor in a business building between Roswell and West Wieuca in North Buckhead/Sandy Springs. I added a wall mural in the waiting area with the com-pany's logo along with the décor. The estimated total was a little over $26,000.

Thank God for the help of Direct. I was up and running within five weeks. It was like a dream come true. The last two weekends before the grand opening, the boys were finally able to visit. They were able to see some of this process firsthand, instead of what they heard from third-party haters.

Direct stepped up more than I ever expected when I had to work from home. He took care of the salon contractors, and he called me on FaceTime to make sure things were just as I needed them. I worked six days a week during this time, taking fifteen clients each day.

The amount of love I received was breathtaking. Even with my charging a travel fee, these ladies tipped above 15-18 percent of the service price. I couldn't count how many times I received congratulations.

Their words weighed so heavily. They were implanted in my mind as I slept, giving me the best energy when I woke up, regardless of how tired I was.

It helped replace the words I wasn't hearing from my own mom and family. Before I decided to work from home and provide mobile services, I asked my mom if I could work from the shop a couple days out of the week. It would have helped me so much to be in on location.

She said, "I don't have the parking space or the space in the salon around my clientele."

I would have rather she told me no. The reasons were bullshit. She made me feel like I was the competitor not only from that incident alone. We couldn't even have a conversation about new techniques in the industry without her becoming defensive. So, out of respect, I left it alone. It wasn't like I came from a "know-it-all" or "listen to me, I know more" place. I wanted to share what I learned with her because I wanted us both to be current with all the new techniques. The industry changes so much.

My mother wasn't a high school graduate and made a life for herself from pure hustle. She was stuck in a dead-end pattern in comparison to the industry, and I didn't want that for her. The products had and were constantly changing. The applications and terminology were changing. If it took me going to school to help her catch up to the current techniques for our family's legacy, that's what I had done, and I thought she would see it that way.

At the end of the day, she was my mom. I loved her to no end, and it was the least I could do, given that she inspired me to be in this industry. She took the lack of support she received from her mom and just generously passed it down to me, doing the family legacy a complete disservice. I learned that it would be hard to have a healthy relationship with her at any point, but why was it that way?

I knew anything related to generational curse-breaking was very difficult, but that's a real understatement. I literally saw how I became cringy to people I knew all my life. It was disturbing to see. I wanted to apply common sense to life more than what we all knew and understood—more rights than lefts, more wins than losses, more blessings than curses.

The boys' last weekend with me was the salon's grand opening. It was nothing minus grace that the schedule stayed as planned. The day of the grand opening was the first time the boys met Direct. I knew I took a chance adding this introduction in a day not knowing the outcome, but the workload was so hectic. It was the only window because in my free time (which was bare), the boys had my undivided attention so we were able to catch up.

Direct and I worked hard for this day. Both of us were on Live, sharing the moment with those who weren't able to come to the event. We only invited thirty people, our heaviest supporters. It was an event full of smiles, laughs, and positive vibes, and the boys were so happy to be there.

LaTrey said, "I heard you weren't goin' open the salon, this is a big day for Momma."

Kingdom added, "I did too, bruh."

"Oh, no. We are not bringing up what we heard today. Thank God for the words spoken over my life and I appreciate him for that man he put in my life for helping with this moment 'cause I am open, baby!" I wrapped my arms around Direct's waist and placed my head on the top of his stomach below his chest.

Since the boys mentioned that aloud, I had to reset the energy in the room. Positive vibes only!

I looked up at Direct, initiating him to toast with me. "Thank you, Papi, for all your help. WE DID IT!"

Prai and Foreign both showed up and showed out with the gift cards from beauty supply, grocery, and other retail stores. A lot of my invites were so excited to meet Direct, after hearing and only seeing him all over my social media pages for months.

Prai said, "Finally, the man of Parys's hour. It is so nice to meet you. You make my friend so happy."

"That's my baby. I love her for real, dog. I'm glad

she opened up to me in multiple ways." They laughed and fist-bumped each other.

While I'd started and finished things before, I'd never done anything of this magnitude. I couldn't compare my successes to my grandmother or my mom. I was in a different era. I received recognition and love from complete strangers from the Internet watching me build my business from the bottom up. I looked around the room at everyone smiling and celebrating my accomplishment. I realized I was able to have great success because those individuals that surrounded me supported me to its fruition. I finally understood how the baddies on IG felt. I was one of the IG baddies now with 50k followers on IG, 15k subscriptions on YouTube, and 30k on TikTok.

It wasn't easy. I had issues in my life I needed to address, but having a supportive man, my boys, and friends during this process was all I needed to get me through. I was finally able to have people I could trust to share my vision when I wanted to vent, while they in return encouraged and pushed me through moments of anxiety.

I finally understood how the girls could sit in their groups and post those lit brunch pictures on IG. How you could feel the love via pictures. I saw how having that strong circle was significant in success of any sort. I mean, Jesus did heal a paralyzed man because of what his friends believed. It helped soothe the pain of my mom not showing up to be here. "I got to work" was her excuse yet again for not being able to make it to what I invited her too. It was cool. With my boys on my right and my man on my left, we all collectively cut the ribbon with smiles as the pictures were taken.

The hearts flooded both of our social media pages. I cried the entire time, and Foreign cussed me out for having to touch me up for pictures.

"Girl, I really beat your face today. Stop crying. I know you happy, but damn," she complained as she sprayed more setting spray.

Chapter Seven

After the grand opening, Direct chilled with the boys. Surprisingly, they gravitated toward him without too much restriction or hesitation, happy about the new Js he brought them. The little asses was going to like the love he showed; I could tell. They also thought he was funny, which helped the icebreaker.

After the grand opening I was having a meeting with Prai and Foreign to review the details and budget for the bridal spa party. I scheduled for us to work the following week. As we talked, a knock sounded at the door.

"Hey, my name is Sean. I own the hair salon a couple doors down. I've heard a lot of great things about you. I looked on your social media and noticed you service Nicki Minaj frequently."

"Yes, I have been." I smiled shyly, stepping into the doorway.

"I have a special client that I would like to refer to you. I already told her you would call her, but she needs you to service her in the next couple hours before an event she is attending."

"In the next couple of hours? Um..."

"It's Marjorie Harvey."

"Excuse me?" I looked at him like a liar I didn't know. "Wow, that's a serious name drop."

"I hate to do this to you. I just didn't want you to second-guess taking the short-notice request, possibly missing the opportunity. Can you call her as soon as you're able?" Holding his hand out for my phone to enter her contact information for me.

"Sure. Let her know I'm in a meeting, but I will be done in twenty minutes. Then, I will call her."

"Thank you so much. I'm sorry it's last minute, but I want her to have the best service available. They just moved to Atlanta a couple months ago. It's a good time to retain her as a client."

I returned to the meeting, my face flushed in pecan brown.

Prai asked, "What's wrong, sis? You OK?"

"Yeah," I mumbled, still in shock and nervous to say the client's name out loud. "I have to call Marjorie Harvey to schedule her for this evening."

Prai and Foreign squealed. "Yes, bitch!" They

jumped up and down, hugging and kissing me all over my face.

"That's amazing, Parys. Oh my God! Baby, that's the ticket."

Direct walked in with the boys. "What's the ticket?"

"The salon neighbor referred Marjorie Harvey to me to service her this evening."

My boys sang in sync: "Momma!" LaTrey pulled his ice cream from his face with his eyes bulging.

Direct pulled me to him, hugging me with a slight rock and kissing my forehead. "You that it girl. I'm so happy for you. That's so good. You need me to take the boys to my place or yours?"

Kingdom chimed in, "I want to see where you stay."

"Let me finish with Prai and Foreign. I'll pack my things after I call her, service her, and meet y'all back at your spot."

"You better work," he said, a little sassy, and he looked over at Prai. "That was decent? Not too zesty but boyfriend-supportive enough, right?"

Prai laughed. "You so funny. It was definitely boyfriend-supportive."

"I'm the cool boyfriend. We are all a family now! Like, for real, I appreciate y'all being here for me and my angel. We making it, y'all. We making it!" He tried to produce fake tears.

"Um, Papi, get your ass out of here," I said as I

pushed him toward the door. "I got this meeting to finish."

"OK, loveface. You know I get wrapped up."

Foreign giggled. "Direct is a mess."

We quickly wrapped up the meeting, allowing me time to calm my nerves and get thoughts together to call Marjorie. I said a quick prayer before I picked up the phone and dialed her. After this call, my name in this industry would be solidified.

"Good evening. How are you? This is the lash tech, Parys."

"Yes. I was expecting your call. Are you available in the next hour? I have an engagement to attend."

"Yes. Sean told me. I made necessary arrangements to be available for you. I included the last-minute price and travel fee included in the service I'm requesting the payment via Apple Pay."

"That's not a problem. Let me send you my address, and I will see you soon."

I had to present myself in a more polished way, knowing this was not Nicki. Marjorie was mature and sophisticated, and while she was cool, her true personality wasn't as publicly known as Nicki's was. I wanted to get to know her a little better. However, she caught a little of my personality responding to her question.

She asked, "You know what you're doing, right?"

"Well, I was referred to you for the best service

and experience and this is Atlanta. I have never lost a client, only gained them." It was a natural response, I wanted to add that I serviced Nicki, but I withheld.

Marjorie chuckled in response, "Alright now."

On my way to Marjorie's, I FaceTimed Direct.

He asked, "How you feel? Did you get another bottle of water before you left the shop?"

"Yes, I did. I feel fine. It's another client to service. I'm goin' in here, doing my thing, getting my money, and leaving."

"You realize you goin' to Steve Harvey's house, right? That nigga *rich* rich. It's another ball game. Nicki had you at one of her condos here in the city, not the house in the hills in LA, so this will be different. This is like goin' from the mayor's condo to the White House. Baby, be ready. Don't have your goofy ass in there nervous, but be aware you are on some next-level shit. Your talents deserve to be on this level. Know you are that bitch. Are you doing a Boomerang for your IG Story?"

"Baby, I don't know. I'm waiting to get there and catch the vibe first. You know I want to, but I don't know if I should 'cause I don't need them haters on my ass."

"Parys, fuck them folks. Don't think about them at all. That's goin' slow you down, and that's really what they want."

"OK. I'm pulling up to the gate call box. Let me call you back once I'm done."

I was at Steve Harvey's house. I heard Drake's "Started from the Bottom" in my head as I drove up. My stomach was spinning. I was glad I still had my makeup on and was dressed from the grand opening, so I wasn't meeting this lady half-assed.

Walking up to the door—the door was so fucking big, like big—it opened, and the housekeeper instructed me that Mrs. Harvey was upstairs waiting for me in her spa room. She asked if I wanted to take the stairs or the elevator and reached for my roller bag.

"I would like the elevator, please." There was no way I was going to pass up the opportunity of getting on the elevator in the Harvey home. I stepped off the elevator, calmed my face, and walked into the room.

"Good evening, Mrs. Harvey. How are you?"

"Please call me Marjorie. How are you doing? I have a chaise chair we can work on. Let me know what you need." She directed me to the space where she wanted to be serviced.

I was nervous all of a sudden. I had never been in a house so nice in all my life. My mom used to service Sleepy Brown's wife from Organized Noise when I grew up, so I was over there often. LaTrey even played with his boys, but that was a mini-mansion. Nothing like Harvey's home.

This house was, if I had to guess, well over 15,000 square feet, detailed with elegant décor. I could only imagine waking up to this every morning. It would be a dream come true if I lived in a home of this magnitude. From the fresh flowers to the décor, the air smelled rich, as if worry or stress was scared to come on their street. It wasn't a social media moment. It was a moment to give Marjorie the best me, the version of myself I wanted to be a year from now. It was the most focused I ever was with a client. I finished within an hour and a half to make sure she stayed on her schedule.

Leaving there, I continuously thanked God for sending another woman to help show me the next level I needed to apply to better myself. I immediately called Direct.

He answered, "Sexy, you good? Where you at?"

"Yeah, I'm good. We got money to make, I see."

"You just now figured that out? That shit was bussing, wasn't it? Steve was there? You mention me?"

"How the boys doing? I'm on my way."

"Yeah, they on the game giving me hell. The boys cool as hell, for real. Lady, answer my questions. I was checking on your page. I ain't see you load up the move."

"I didn't. I honestly didn't want to. I need Marjorie to call me again. I was a little overwhelmed. It was a great experience, Papi—a real dream. Their home is absolutely beautiful. I ain't goin' lie. I got nervous once I was about to start, so I had to stay focused. We small-talked. I wanted to feel her vibe. I was focused as fuck. So, no, I didn't mention you or anything about me personally."

"I can understand that. You know, you got to get used to that. Once I start the tour with the guys, I need you on the road a little bit so you goin' be on the scene. This is your new life. That old shit done."

And he was not lying. I was so busy during the next two months. I won an international lash competition, worked with models at hair shows in the city, and collaborated with Danessa Myricks as well as a variety of well-known salons in the city. I also had the opportunity to service Sheryl Lee Ralph and attend several celebrity parties in the city.

I was busy to the point that Jared and Keith complained about me being too caught up in my career, only allowing me two weekends to see the boys since the salon opening. If it was ever a push or argument to get them, I didn't force the visit. The drama distracted from the progress I made at the salon and the relationships I was building with Nicki, Marjorie, and her entourage of friends.

Direct and I both agreed it was best I ignored the drama with the boys. I hated that I offered up my boys as a sacrifice to establish the consistency needed for my career. That led to countless nights of crying and heated arguments between Direct and me. We always worked it out, but it happened often.

Looking back, I felt like we had to release that frustration so he could have a better understanding about how I saw things and the way I wanted things to pan out for the future. It was so embarrassing to log on to the Internet and see someone calling me an unfit mom or have my past dug up and mentioned on their pages. Apparently, I was on a pedestal that haunted them in their sleep, seeing as there was a new post every morning mentioning something old.

One weekend, the boys didn't have clothes with them, and the clothes they had on were nothing I bought them. They were in something you would not come out of the house in.

I picked up the boys outside of my mom's salon. I greeted Keith, "Yo, my guy, why he not dressed? I sent clothes with him last month. Where are they?"

"They are at home. Why? Take them shopping with you and your little lame-ass Internet boyfriend."

I did not respond because it wasn't a problem. They wanted a response from me. He mentioned Direct just to start an argument so I could lower my vibrations to where theirs were. They saw what vibe Direct and I were on and the type of lifestyle we were trying to live.

Direct's platform followers were over 2 million,

and I reached over 100,000 collectively after starting my YouTube lash tutorial channel with over 15,000 subscribers. We were gaining major popularity. Direct even closed an eight-city tour deal with his Internet peers that he advertised with interviews on several local radio stations and podcasts.

Regardless of how long LaTrey and Kingdom were away, Jared and Keith hated to see the unity we had once we got them or the positive response we received from fans in the comments when we posted about the boys periodically. Our bond was solid. Our audience had no indication of the drama, though. The boys spent time with us, and they especially loved spending time with me at the salon.

Hell, LaTrey turned into a photographer. I even taught my baby how to load the pictures on IG with the right filters and all. Kingdom was the flirt, making all the women feel good from the time they walked in until they left. It was cute to see them working with the clients. Kingdom directed the clients on angles, and LaTrey snapped the pictures. Teamwork! I gave them photo and creative director credits every time. It boosted their confidence so when they returned back with their dads, Jared and Keith had to work even harder to tear their confidence back down. It was the only reason I could think of why they made it so hard for me to have the boys on more weekends. But they returned to their dad bragging at the end of the weekend every time. That was just going to be how it went for my young kings.

When I vented to Direct, I expressed how hard it was to rebuild the boys' confidence every visit I had with them. I stayed up late some nights, working on my content and booking spa parties, just imagining the mental work they put in to make sure my kids didn't feel like they were worthy of love and attention. It pushed me to a level of anger where I stopped paying my child support payment every month.

I chumped them off just like they were doing with my boys, and Direct supported my decision. It hurt him and made him upset that they were getting done that way. We started making plans on getting a bigger space for them when the following school year came, and we would keep Direct's high rise as an Airbnb investment property.

I had to ask Direct to stop telling the boys our future plans, as the information was getting back to the co-parents. They just got together on some occasions to plot bullshit towards me. I only knew this information from the boys telling me how they would see each other outside of their weekend visits with me. It was such an unsolved mystery, how their shared hate for me brought about so much unity. I understood Direct wanting to assure the boys that they were included and we were making plans for them, but when they went back home, it was like the information was tortured out of them just so the co-parents could be up to date on my goals for what reason I don't know they weren't benefiting.

Direct and I started finding real humor in what we heard from the boys. I remembered laughing about it one night.

"You a baddie, little momma. They goin' make me start adding this in the content so they can see how stupid they look."

I think it turned him on that I had this amount of drama surrounding me, judging from how rough the sexual session was that night after the conversation. Purr! Big purr!

The real confirmation of jealousy was the stunt that Adrienne pulled after the third month the salon was open. She saw the success of the salon. I knew she was at her breaking point because she waited until the thirty-first day I was behind on a payment. She took it upon herself to file child abandonment with the courts with a private action for the arrears owed from the months of not receiving the full payment and posted the status to her FB page. This angry lady sent the documents to the salon despite the fact that she had my personal home address, making sure the deputies came to the salon to serve me the papers.

I received the deliveries on two different occasions while I was working. One came on a Tuesday and the other on the following Monday. I was glad the salon wasn't packed on both those days. I let the shit slide that Tuesday, meaning I didn't give them the response and attention they expected. But the following week, oh hell naw! You know I called the house after my last client that day.

"Jared there?"

Adrienne answered. "He ain't here. What's up?"

"What the fuck you on, cunt?"

"You fake-ass mother."

"Look, you jealous-ass bitch, like I asked, what you on? I'm on my way." I grabbed my keys. I was over the acts of kindness. It was time to get active.

"You come over here, you getting locked up."

"Today is my day, ho. Bond money on deck. If I ain't got it, my nigga got it. You know the vibes, dusty-ass bitch."

"That nigga making you. You ain't shit, bitch."

"Oh, that's what you think, you punk-ass bitch. Garbage pail, Sesame Street, trash-can-ass ho. I'm goin' to show you who I am today. I'm on your ass, and I ain't letting up. You've been on my wish list, and this is the day it's goin' be granted."

"Your salon ain't goin' make it a year. You want to be your momma so bad. Be yourself, bitch."

As I stepped off the elevator, my vision blurred. I was so mad. Adrienne's comeback comment about my mom killed my self-conscious. Some of what she said was definitely accurate. I did things for my mom to gain attention and love, just wanting that from her, and Adrienne knew it. I had no option but to fight the bitch. What this gopher-built body-ass girl couldn't clock me on was my skill. And that's what she didn't talk about. I was dominating my lane, winning, getting recognition and respect from the left to the right of the industry, and everybody had access to watch that's where her anger stemmed from.

"Keep that same energy, beaver brain. Matter of fact, where your man at? Fucking on a bad bitch, I hope, and about to bring you that leftover dick. Your thirsty ass licking another bitch's juice from the only dick you can get, slow-ass girl."

I walked out the door to the parking lot, yelling on the phone. Direct was standing there. I completely forgot we planned a date because he was about to go on his tour for a month, leaving in a couple days.

He stopped me. "What's wrong? What's wrong? Where are you goin'?" He tried to stop me from walking to my car. "Answer me," he yelled and reached for my phone. "Give me the phone. Don't argue with nobody. Who is on the phone?"

I don't know why, but I just started swinging on him.

"Give me my fucking phone. I ain't the one. This bitch got me fucked up." I landed at least three punches to his head.

"Parys, if you don't stop hitting me… Baby, please calm down. What happened?" He grabbed me, pinning me to the car hood with all of his weight. I burst into tears.

"She sent the deputy again. I'm tired," I screamed repeatedly.

"Again today, after last week? No, baby, what the fuck?" He hugged me tighter, making sure I didn't move. "I'm sorry, baby. I'm so sorry. I got you. I love you. I'm all you need, I swear. I can't let you fuck up all your hard work."

Sean ran to the parking lot, hearing the screaming from his salon suite, and saw Direct leaned in over me. "She OK? What happened?"

Direct replied, "I got her. Thank you, my dog. I got her."

"Let me know if you need anything."

"Baby, get it together. You've worked too hard to be acting out, in front of these salon suites. Baby, think."

I still cried, loud. I hit my breaking point. It had been so long since I last slapped a bitch.

"Baby, come get in the car, please." He picked me up and sat me in the passenger seat of my car.

"You goin' drive me over there?"

"Girl, no. Your stupid ass ain't spending money on bonding out from nowhere. We can't even do a skit, your face so puffy. Pretty lady, damn! We goin' stay in tonight. I have to take care of your ass 'cause you want to show the fuck out. Oh, you gettin' it rough tonight, little mama."

My head was pounding. I felt sick. As soon as I opened the car door, I vomited.

"Fuck, Parys. You have made yourself sick by being so upset." He held back my thirty-inch extensions. "I can't believe them muthafuckas, petty hos. I got to feed you and get you home."

Adrienne's voice filled the new silence. "Hello?"

"Bitch, your goofy rat-face ass on the phone still." Direct hung up. "Baby, close the door. You think you done?"

Slapping the dashboard, I said, "She was on the line the whole time listening." I was embarrassed at that point, and Direct was embarrassed for me. He felt it, and the look in his eyes showed so much compassion.

"Baby, I love you so much. I got us, all us." His eyes watered as he drove off and made the turn into the Chinese restaurant by the condo. "Baby, I'm goin' get you some hot-and-sour soup and crab rangoon. Papi know what you want. I don't want to leave you and go on this tour, but I have to. We need this."

Once he was out the car, I just started screaming and punching at the dashboard. He quickly ran back to the car.

"Let me just go to the crib. Baby, calm the fuck down. You goin' get yourself sick again. Fuck!" He screamed so loud, louder than I had ever heard his voice reach, especially toward me! Direct pulled in front of the condo, instead of in the parking deck, and led me to the elevators. He stopped at the concierge desk to ask the attendant he was cool with to park the car and hold the key until he returned.

"Parys, come get your ass in the shower, so I can bathe you and you can lie down. I want you to cancel your clients for tomorrow and rest. I don't want to hear shit about it." He gave me a deep stare with tears in his eyes.

"OK, Papi." My embarrassment level was so high. I had no room to argue.

Thankfully, I only had four clients to reschedule. It was a walk-in day, so I would only miss the surprise money. I was in no mental position to pour energy into anyone, and my man was leaving the following night. We literally had one full day to spend together.

My clients had grown to be some of the most loyal people I had ever met in my life. Of course, I discounted 10 percent off their service price for the inconvenience, but they understood the reason I gave them. It was the first time I called out for work, owning my own salon. I felt guilty because I knew people wanted to know that they could rely on their tech. Calling out with less than twenty-four hours' notice was not building the reputation of dependability.

I lay in bed with the most intrusive thoughts, like I had to do better if I wanted to be a successor to my mom or even Rachel. This move wasn't pushing me in that direction. Thinking about that made me even madder at the distraction from this child support situation. But then, I thought, *Should I let that be a distraction?* I was so weak for letting the tactic affect me.

Direct noticed the look on my face when he walked in the room with food that was delivered.

"Parys, get the fuck out of your head. Damn, girl, sit up so you can eat. You did what I asked you to do?"

"Don't I always?"

"You better. Look, you got me feeling weird about leaving you, and you got this shit goin' on and court coming up. I need you on your beat long enough to make it to Jacksonville for the second show. Parys, promise me you are goin' be there. Don't let me down. It's goin' mess up my focus and energy if you up here making emotional decisions, responding to the BS they throwing at you. You in here all over the place now, and I had three skits for us to do."

"Papi, no, I got it! We can do the skits. I can put some shades on and do what I have to. I'm sorry. She called my stupid today."

"Oh, she accomplished her goal for sure. Don't be sorry, though. To be honest, you should have fought her years ago, so she would know how to move now, but that's what you get for being nice and shit. Sometimes, fuck being the bigger person. You have to check shit on sight."

"But—"

"No buts, Parys. Go ahead and eat, so we can get to work."

"OK."

After a day of rest and spending time with Direct, I had a weird feeling but thought it was because I missed Direct already, as he walked into the airport doors. Driving from the airport, I wondered whether I wanted to sleep at his place for emotional comfort or go back to my place to finish scheduling the remainder of my month before I went into the salon early the following morning. A thought crossed my mind.

When was my period supposed to come this month? Was I late? I thought maybe I should stop at the store on my way to get a pregnancy test. I calculated the weeks and realized I was at least two weeks late. It could be stress. I had a lot going on.

I returned to the condo, went straight to the bathroom, and took the test. As I stared at it, waiting for the results, I received a FaceTime call from Direct.

I answered, "Hey, bae, you made it to the gate?"

"Yeah. What are you doing?"

"About to floss and brush you out my mouth," I replied, wanting to keep it spicy to distract from the fact I looked like I'd hit a line of coke from a Colombian cartel lab.

"Don't start, don't start. OK, then, go ahead and get some rest. I'm goin' call you when I land in a couple hours. You lock the door?"

"You know I locked the door. You are so overprotective."

"That's what I'm supposed to be about you."

"Yes, I know, baby, and thank you. Go ahead and get your flight. Call me once you land."

"OK. Love you."

"I love you too."

I disconnected the call. I looked down and saw a pink cross. I didn't know what to say or how to feel. LaTrey was twelve, and Kingdom was almost nine. Who wanted to start over? I didn't want to call Direct right back to share the news. I honestly thought to keep the information to myself, listening to the devil on my left shoulder. He was on tour for almost a month. I had enough time to handle this my way. I just had to put it in a schedule, using those time management skills I was so blessed to have.

I stood in a daze, trying to figure out how I got in this predicament. It wasn't the time for a baby. My career was just doing what it needed to do. Yeah, yeah, yeah, I was on cowgirl time a lot, but that was Papi. Who else was going to get it? He wasn't having nothing less, but he pulled out way more than he stayed stuck in.

I shouldn't have been surprised. I started to listen to the angel on my right, telling me we made a love child. I deserved a fresh start and a new beginning. Direct wanted to be with me forever, share the news. We could gain so much social media attention from taking our relationship into a new level. Who knew? Maybe we could get sponsored for our wedding. Wait, wedding?! I didn't know how in the hell I ventured off that deep. I said to myself, "Parys, stop being delusional. This is not a fairytale love story." I pondered my next move while I posted the testimonial sent to me that morning on my IG:

Wow, I love them! They look so natural. I love waking up in the morning and looking like a million bucks! My light eyelashes were barely visible without mascara. Now they look great, even when I just get out of the shower and haven't put my makeup on yet. I feel beautiful all the time! Parys has made my morning routine simpler and quicker. My lashes look long, full, and fabulous. Thanks!

—Marjorie Harvey

When I was looking at my schedule and realized I was booked out for three months outside of walk-in days at the salon. I thought, now that's content for a post, let me share the news and opening up a waitlist. Posting another testimony after Majorie's:

Hello, Parys,

My name is Isheia, and you did my eyebrows before in Atlanta. I called the number on the card you gave me while you were in school, and I had no success. I wanted to know if you still did eyebrows. If so, I would love for you to do mine. I love the way you did them. No one has come close! If this email reaches you, let me know. Either way, you were great at your craft, so I hope you are.

Direct's career was also taking off. No way I would stop his journey. He was not ready for a baby. I thought about it for the following week, while I was working, continuing my everyday routine. I was so on the fence about when I would tell Direct about the pregnancy. It was like he knew something was different about the way I acted toward him.

First, I thought about starting an argument with him, but that was stupid and really not my character. I would have felt like shit disturbing his peace while he was on the grind and, from what I could see, being loyal to our relationship. I was quieter than normal during our FaceTime calls, not really looking in the camera when we spoke.

"Babe, what's been the problem? I told you I have to move with the group, so if we are at the strip club, I have to be there. And you know I'm goin' throw money with the guys."

"Babe, I'm not thinking about that. You know my court appearance is coming up, and I had to reschedule Marjorie to be there. I'm just annoyed about it."

"Damn, yeah! You are annoyed. It will be over, and then you will be meeting me in Jacksonville on your days off. Right?"

"Correct. I have the schedule worked out to be there for a couple days like we planned. I just feel so out of sorts having to rearrange my business to entertain the trash shit these people are on with me."

"I know it is some deadbeat shit, but it's life right now. It's one day to get behind you. What does your schedule look like for the rest of this week?"

"I got the wedding party and Nicki outside of the salon schedule. I'm editing the video I did last night to load on YouTube in a minute."

"Yeah, that last one you looked so good on. You had a little extra glow on that one. What filter was that?" We both laughed.

"No filter. That was that new ring light I just got." Damn, this man saw his baby through the camera. I got him off the phone quickly after that comment. "Babe, let me call Prai and make sure he got the other table for the event. He training a new person coming in."

"Not expansion."

"Expansion, baby."

I really got off the phone to leave another voicemail with the clinic to schedule an appointment before I traveled to see him in another week.

During Nicki's appointment, I got too comfortable mentioning I had court in a couple days, and I didn't feel like going.

"What you got court for?"

"A child support case."

"Oh, they mad you making your coin," she

snickered with laughter. "They really would be mad if they knew you were doing Nicki Minaj like you do. You really are sparing their feelings. You don't post every move. You are a little humble. I get it. They can't count everything, you know."

"Exactly what I be thinking, and I don't like my money being counted at all."

"Broke bitches do that or try to. They can't keep up. Don't even worry about it. Do your thing."

I laughed, loving her Caribbean accent. "Oh, I am."

Leaving Nicki's that night, I experienced all types of emotions about my current circumstance. I knew this pregnancy was causing me to overthink about things like the relationship with my mom, the drama with my boys' fathers, the increase in clients at the salon, my online popularity, and my relationship with Direct. It was so much to juggle, but somehow, I was doing it! I just needed to push a little harder and a little longer. Things would most definitely get better or better to manage. If I could get past this court appearance and confirm a date with this clinic before I saw Direct, it would be a true sign God was smiling.

The morning of my court appearance, I just stayed on my routine of prayer, meditation, yoga, and whatever I could stomach to eat for the morning with my daily vitamins. Direct called.

"Good morning, Papi! I'm surprised you up. I followed your Story last night."

"Loveface, you know I have to keep up with the guys on this road. They were talking trash to me about being in the club texting with you last night, but it was just fun. I'm not and would not cheat on you."

"To be fair, I wouldn't know, so I can't think too far into it to care."

"Damn, Parys. You on one this morning, but you ready for the day."

"Yes, mentally I am. I have to make sure I get Prai and Foreign in the hotel suite for the spa party scheduled. I should get there no later than one."

"What you eat this morning? I'm goin' DoorDash you something."

"You didn't spend it all last night?"

"Parys, stop it. I threw maybe a thousand. That has nothing to do with what I do for you, and that's nothing in comparison to what I have spent on you."

"You right, Papi. I'm goin' get on your case about it, though. Incidents like that get rumors started. I don't want to be one of those falling Internet couples. And I don't want to keep up with a positive image or reputation in public when I'm taking disrespect privately."

"You leaving from the rise or the apartment?"

"Apartment."

"Why? You didn't want to be at the rise leaving for court this morning? It's closer."

"Well, Papi, I had Nicki last night, and what I wanted to wear was at the apartment."

"Loveface, I'm goin' get you the biggest crib the budget can buy. I don't want you worrying about nothing but your salon, your clients, me, and the boys. You don't really sound like yourself, but I can't worry too much. I just sent you a Cash App for wherever you want for breakfast or lunch when you leave."

I stopped at a light to check my phone. "Direct, why are you so extra? $500."

"Treat your team today, loveface."

"Aw, thank you, Papi! I will! Trying to keep me off your case, I see."

"A brother gotta do what he has to do. We damn near stay together. I got to get back home. You don't have too much longer before you come to see me."

"Yes, I'm looking forward, but, baby, let me speed up this process and get to this courthouse."

"OK. I love you, Parys," he screamed so loud I could hear his friends in the background telling him to shut up.

Laughing, I said, "Since you woke everyone up, tell them I said hello."

"I will. Call me when you leave, like as soon as."

"I know. I will. I love you too."

Walking into the courthouse texting in a group chat with Prai and Foreign.

Parys: "Did the front desk have your name added to get a key to the suite?"

Foreign: "Yes, I got there before Prai and just told him to come up to meet me."

Parys: "I confirmed eight out of the ten last night. The room should be decorated already. I just need you to let the catering company up when they get there."

Prai: "I was running behind. There was an accident this morning, and I almost had to read the cake lady picking up the dessert platter."

Parys: "Baby, let's not burn that bridge too early 'cause I haven't found her a replacement yet."

Prai: "They were a little dry to me last time."

Foreign: "I thought it was just me."

Parys: "Hell, I wouldn't know. I haven't had a taste for sweets lately. My body on summertime fine. I'm focused lol."

I quickly glanced up to make sure I was headed in the right direction. I saw a girl I went to high school with as our eyes caught one another.

"Heyyyy…" I tried to remember her name.

"Tracey, Nicole's best friend."

"Yes, it's been so long. How have you been? Take my IG."

"Oh, no! I follow you on Facebook and IG. You are doing so good. You look amazing! I've been trying to figure out a time to schedule with you, waiting on my brows to grow out."

"Thank you so much. You are so sweet. Definitely let me know. Well, it was good to see you."

We parted ways. I noticed she had a badge on, but I didn't get into the detail as the folders she held obstructed the title. I carried on down the hall into the room to find a seat. There was Jared and Adrienne in the second or third aisle from the front of the courtroom, turned around as if they were waiting for me to walk in the courtroom. They quickly turned around once they saw me and began to whisper with their attorney as she went to walk toward the bailiff.

I didn't want to focus on what they were doing as I needed to check on Prai and Foreign before I turned off the phone. Court was about to start.

"All rise."

I saw Tracey walk in with Jared's attorney. I didn't want to speculate what they were doing. I didn't know and couldn't put my finger on it. Once court began, the bailiff walked over to me.

"Are you Parys Germane?"

"I am."

"I need you to come with me."

"May I ask why?" I asked with a slightly confused smile.

"You have a warrant for your arrest."

"Warrant? Come again?" My eyes popped out of my head while I maintained my winning-hand poker face.

"Yes I need you to come with me." I stood up. "Can you turn around and put your hands behind your back?"

My soul ran out the room, as I turned around slowly, doing everything I could not to look at Jared and Adrienne.

As I sat in the cold jail cell waiting to be called into the courtroom to appear before the judge, I thought, *Parys, what could you have done differently? What could you have said to make your baby daddy and his wife like or accept you enough to keep them from going to such extreme measures?* Why should I have had to do anything else but be myself? I was never disrespectful or threatening toward their union.

I hoped this bullshit would be over soon. I would hate to lose everything I worked for. It took me so long to build my business and establish my name in my industry. I just knew once I went back in the courtroom, the judge would hear both sides, have me pay a little fine, or give me another court date so I could get back to building my business. I didn't need any type of major setback to happen now.

Little did I know, walking back into the courtroom, that would not be the case. If I could have twinkled my nose to make myself invisible or became a smoke cloud to avoid that walk of shame, I would have. They placed me at the podium, wearing my high-waisted dress pants with my long-sleeved satin bodysuit. The shackles around my Tom Ford padlock pointed toe pumps was not the look I was going for that day. I heard someone's camera flash go off in the background.

"Can you loosen up my ankle cuffs a little? I promise I'm not running."

"Sure. The more you move, the tighter they will get."

The judge spoke then. "Ms. Germane, it was brought to the court's attention that you had a warrant for failure to appear at your court appearance yesterday."

"Excuse me, can I speak?"

"Sure. What would you like to share?"

"I missed an appearance yesterday, and I came today. Why would I do that? I'm confused."

"I was confused as well, but by law, I have to sentence you, forty-five days mandatory for the missed court appearance."

"Your honor, I can't do forty-five days. I have a

business to run. I have clients scheduled for the next ninety days. I'm booked."

"I can understand the inconvenience this will cause you. However, my hands are tied due to the warrant that was issued. You will be kept in custody until you serve the forty-five days. Then your new court date will be generated after time is served, and we will then address the matters on the case today."

She banged the gavel, ruling the judgment. My heart coated my stomach like acid. I walked past Jared and Adrienne as they glanced back with looks of victory as the day turned into a blur.

The guard yelled at me to back up. Direct stood tall, looking down at me as I was buzzed out of my pod. I walked up the stairs slowly, in absolute embarrassment. Direct had a gentle smile with his sad eyes. I knew I had a lot of explaining to do. I picked up the phone as tears filled his gaze. He looked at me as if he was trying to read my mind for the answers to his questions.

"Baby, what the fuck? Like, baby, what are we goin' do? Have you thought about your clients? The salon? Nicki and Marjorie? What about your place? You know we have to stay on social media. Our last two videos are at almost half a million views on YouTube. We need to have a lawyer come see you. You need me to get your property from here? There is a form you have to sign to release it to me. I asked when I arrived. I don't want your stuff in here. How long they say you gotta be here? It's been eight days already. You know that's too long, right? Say something, baby! Why are you just staring at me?"

"I'm waiting on—"

"I need you to call me. Why you ain't call me? I can't sleep like that, not with you being in here. You know I called the court clerk the next day when I didn't hear from you? I'm missing two shows tonight 'cause I had to come see you when the visitation clearance got approved. I haven't been to my crib yet. I came straight here. I leave back out tonight. I left Cincinnati this morning at eight. Baby, I ain't sleep with nobody. I go to the club for the pictures and shit, but, girl, I've been sick about you. Like, I really love us." He slapped the phone on the wall. "Girl, say something. I'm pouring out my fucking heart. I ain't never felt this way." A tear fell down his cheek.

"Direct, I'm pregnant." I stared at him with a face full of tears. "I'm so sorry for doing this to us." I released a cry filled with the most pain Direct had ever heard me express towards him. "Direct, I'm sorry!

I'm so sorry. I'm pregnant! We don't have to keep it. We don't. I will be out of here in time, and we can go handle things. Look, I really respect the fact that you have made decisions for your life that didn't involve carelessness. You were a ho in the streets but a careful one, you know? You didn't involve yourself in spontaneous, irrational decisions to stay in something warm for another forty-five secs, not even on your most faded night, and I give you your flowers for that. Your career status, my career status, mixed with this shit," I pointed at my stomach, "I don't think it needs to happen. I got too much personal drama goin' on for me to focus on a baby. I need to get my shit together cause this ain't it." Tears flowed down my face like the Yellowstone flowing into the Missouri River. "I need some time. You don't deserve to have all this attached to you. Baby, I will be too occupied with cleaning up my past choices. It's goin' take some serious-ass attention. Love, this ain't for you. We need to take some time apart from one another."

"Wait! I hear what you are saying, doll face, and I respect your respect. But we are on the Internet. We," he gestured between us, "together, the long way now. Parys, our platforms are about to go up!" He wiped his tears in laughter with a beautiful glow coming off his smile. "Girl, I love you! It's us and that baby just confirmed. It's up. Don't think the way you are thinking. You have a lot of negative-ass energy around you in this jail, so you have to stay on ice so you don't upset my baby."

"Um, Direct, I need you thinking—"

The guard indicated we only had five more minutes. Direct nodded in understanding. "Parys, I'm goin' be right here." He pointed at my forehead through the glass window. "I don't have a lot of time. Call me tonight. I added the collect call coverage to my service the second day I knew you were in here. Look, say this number."

"I can't remember all them numbers. You know everything I have to think about? One sec." I turned around to look at the guard. "Can you write this number down for me?"

The guard responded, "What is it, baby momma?"

Direct started laughing hysterically while saying, "I know that's right, Parys. That's my baby. She go make 'em work. 404-639-7116."

"I was thinking 1761. Babe, you know we don't know numbers. That's what the phone's for."

"I know. I land in the morning at five, so call me when you get a chance. No matter where I am, I will pick up the phone. Whatever is goin' on when you call is goin' on pause for fifteen minutes. They told me we can do something like Zoom calls, so at least I can see your face and check on you and the baby. You're pregnant with my baby, barb!"

He gave me the biggest smile. The guard leaned in with the final tap, informing Direct his time was up.

"Hey, loveface, I love you so much! We gonna get through this and figure it out 'cause your baby daddies, your exes, did this because they mad at you. This ain't about the boys." He stood up. "They got you up to your lashes in child support, but I LOVE YOU!" He gently sat the phone receiver on the hook and blew me a kiss, making the biggest heart with his hands.

I couldn't lie. I wanted to mentally teleport through the glass and kiss this man from the top of his dreads to the bottom of his feet because my man, my man, my man! I watched him walk away until he was completely out of the door, knowing it would be a minute before I saw his physical body and our video calls started.

Walking down the steps back toward my pod dorm, I reflected on our visit. Questions ran through my mind. *What just happened to my life? Why haven't I woken up from this nightmare yet? Did Direct just cancel my summer? Will I be home by summer? Wait, fall. Why didn't we talk about a lawyer? That visit was completely unproductive, given the topic at hand. What is the status of my bond? Do I have a bond? What is my social media status? What do my clients think? Has anyone stopped by the salon?*

Direct's habit of twenty questions was rubbing off. God, our energies were starting to sync as I lightly shook my head. *Wait, did he really confirm that I have been here for eight days? What are my children thinking? I know they tried to call me, right?* Nah, their dads probably didn't even let them use the phone, so they were more than likely puzzled as to why I hadn't reached out.

As I stood at the door waiting to get buzzed in, I turned around to the guard. "What's the phone schedule?"

"The pods alternate free time, hour rotates between pods, so it depends on when y'all are out that day. I think y'all out tomorrow morning."

"Why are we on twenty-three hours of lock down? What did somebody do that got us all suffering?"

"Those are the rules, baby momma. It's been twenty-three and one since I've been here the last four years. I'm goin' give you that number when I give you your prenatal vitamin during med call. Make sure you wake up. You can't sleep the time away."

"Shit, sleep keeps my mind from thinking too long 'cause I can't accept the fact that the life I was creating was just daylight robbed from me." I stepped into the pod, and the door closed behind me.